Welcome to Hard Times

An Occasional Paper

Welcome to Hard Times

The Fiscal Consequences of German Unity

ULLRICH HEILEMANN

and

WOLFGANG H. REINICKE

*HJ
2109
.H45
1995*

The Brookings Institution
and
American Institute for Contemporary German Studies at
The Johns Hopkins University
Washington, D.C.

Foreword

Many industrialized countries have confronted serious economic challenges during the past several years, but Germany has encountered unique problems generated by unification. The massive transfer of funds to the eastern part of Germany has increased government deficit spending significantly. To finance these transfers, the German government has imposed tax increases and has sought to cut expenditures, yet government debt still has risen to its highest level in postwar history. While the German economy now seems to be picking up speed, there are still serious challenges to meet if Germany is to secure economic productivity in the future.

The American Institute for Contemporary German Studies at The Johns Hopkins University commissioned Ullrich Heilemann and Wolfgang Reinicke to examine the implications of various policy options for consolidating the federal budget and reducing deficit spending in Germany. They have produced a comprehensive assessment of the German economy, and have provided specific policy recommendations for achieving the goals of economic growth, increased efficiency in the public sector, and deficit reduction. Their study, completed in the fall of 1994, *Welcome to Hard Times: The Fiscal Consequences of German Unity*, contributes to a better understanding of the challenges Germany now faces and can anticipate during the rest of the decade.

This study was made possible by a generous grant from a German financier, Diethelm Höner. The Institute is a private, nonpartisan center for advanced research and study of Germany. The Institute's purposes are to develop a new generation of American scholars with a thorough knowledge of contemporary Germany, to deepen Americans' understanding of the Federal Republic of Germany, and to contribute to the analysis of a broad range of German-American policy problems. The Institute expresses its appreciation to The Brookings Institution for publication of this important study.

The views expressed in this publication are those of the authors and do not necessarily reflect the views of The American Institute for Contemporary German Studies.

Jackson James
Executive Director
AICGS
Washington, D.C.

Lily Gardner Feldman
Research Director
AICGS
Washington, D.C.

Acknowledgements

The authors are grateful to Bernd Fritzsche, Heinz Gebhardt, Hans Dietrich von Loeffelholz, Mathias Moersch, Hermann Rappen, and Joe White for their critical comments. Alexander Ratz and Jim Schoff provided research assistance. Michael Treadway edited the manuscript. Jennifer Mitchell and Christopher Dall provided editorial assistance.

Contents

Introduction and Summary

Unification presents Germany with a series of formidable fiscal challenges in the mid-1990s. Germany has confronted similar challenges in the past, for example during the oil crises of the 1970s, but these were of a temporary nature. The current problems are longer term, because their principal cause—eastern Germany's need for massive fiscal transfers—cannot be expected to abate before the end of the decade. To make matters worse, Germany's new fiscal dilemma comes at a time when the country already faces a number of serious economic challenges: the highest unemployment rate in 35 years; discouraging trends in gross—and in particular net—per capita income; and historically high tax rates, which put Germany at a disadvantage in an increasingly competitive international environment.

Other industrialized countries face similar fiscal and economic difficulties, but Germany's potential to overcome its problems appears much more limited, not only because of the nature and duration of its transfer obligations, but also because of the already high level of taxation. The seriousness of Germany's fiscal challenge has raised deep concerns both within and outside Germany, given its economy's important role both in Europe and abroad.

Initial Conditions

Between 1990 and 1994 western Germany transferred about DM 130 billion, or 5 percent of its GNP, to eastern Germany each year. About DM 40 billion of these transfers, or 1.5 percent of GNP, was financed through government deficits, and the rest by cuts in expenditures (about DM 20 billion), tax increases (about DM 35 billion), and increases in social security contributions (about DM 35 billion). The public share of western German GNP rose from 46 percent in 1990 to 51.5 percent in 1994, and the share of taxes and social security contributions from 40.4 percent to 44.5 percent. The fiscal stimulus from this deficit spending, which was essentially unavoidable, caused Germany's GNP growth to accelerate during 1990 and 1992 by an average of 1.5 to 2.0 percentage points per year. Meanwhile government debt as a share of GNP reached 51.5 percent, its highest level in postwar German history. Inflation increased by about one-third because of the increase in tax rates and government-administered prices. Whether international interest rates rose because of the government deficit is an open question—estimates of the increase vary between 0 and 1.5 percentage points. Whether the German deficit dampened European economic growth also remains undecided, not least because the considerable increase in German imports had an effect counter to that of higher interest rates. It is estimated that this increase in trade increased annual growth rates among the EU economies by between 0.5 and 1 percentage point.

The rising deficits have almost entirely deprived federal, state, and local government budgets of their ability to engage in any kind of expansionary or growth-oriented policy. Already in 1994, interest on the public debt will account for more than 11.4 percent of expenditures, while public investment will amount to only 7.5 percent. Moreover, given the current fiscal outlook there is a widespread fear that tax rates will remain high. Finally, real per capita net income in western Germany, in particular for those who must pay social security contributions, will be scarcely higher in 1994 than in 1989.

Current Perspectives

Even from a medium-term perspective, Germany's macroeconomic and fiscal prospects are not very encouraging. Until 1997, according to current forecasts, western German growth will not exceed 2.5 percent per year; indeed, federal fiscal planners forecast growth of only 1.5 percent. This means not only that unemployment will remain stagnant, but also, with population rising, that real per capita income will grow at best at 1 percent per year. Given the planned increases in taxes and social security contributions, real per capita net income may actually stagnate or decline. The government's fiscal plan calls for the deficit to decrease as a share of GNP from 4.5 percent in 1993 to 1.8 percent by 1997. Meanwhile the debt-GNP ratio will decline only modestly from 60 percent to 56 percent—a level still unprecedented in the pre-1990 history of the Federal Republic.

From an international perspective, Germany's fiscal situation continues to appear favorable. Although the country will lose its long-held lead within the European Union with respect to the deficit and debt ratios, the government expects to fall short of the fiscal criteria established by the Maastricht Treaty only in 1994 (for the deficit) and in 1995 (for the debt).[1] Between 1990 and 1994 external government debt increased by 4 percentage points, to 25 percent of total government debt—a level that still compares favorably with those of other countries. The term structure of the debt has not changed significantly since the mid-1980s and is unlikely to present a problem in the foreseeable future.

However, the price for the rapid deficit reduction envisioned by the government will be high: until 1997 expenditure growth will have to remain more than 2.5 percentage points below the growth of nominal GNP. Given that eastern Germany's transfer needs will remain high for the time being, and that they must be met to sustain the adjustment process, *western* Germany will experience on average nominally stagnant or even declining government expenditures.

Planned expenditure cuts focus on personnel compensation, subsidies, unemployment-related spending, and family, social, and educational support. In the area of social spending the intent is to reduce benefits by aligning them more closely with the income levels of the beneficiaries. On the investment side, major cuts are planned in federal spending for local transport, student loans, defense, residential construction subsidies, the relocation of the federal government to Berlin, and other areas. Investment spending is expected to be reduced from 14.8 percent to 13.1 percent of total expenditures, and a still more significant reduction of investments will take place at the local level. Both reductions, which are anything but attractive from a growth perspective, are rendered necessary by an increase in public consumption expenditures, in particular interest payments and additional allocations, for example to the Debt Redemption Fund (*Erblastentilgungsfond*) and the pension insurance fund. Additional revenues are expected from a reduction in tax abuse and evasion.

The public share of GNP is expected to increase from 45 percent in 1989 to 50 percent in 1997. The GNP share of social security contributions will rise from 17.2 percent to 20 percent, and that of taxes from 23 percent to 26 percent, 2 percentage points (DM 80 billion) of which will be in the form of hidden taxes (i.e., bracket creep—tax brackets in Germany are not indexed to inflation), although this may change depending on the outcome of income tax reform in 1995.

Private households, businesses, and the international community will be affected in different ways by these policies. The expenditure cuts will have their greatest impact on private households. Given the regressive nature of most of these cuts, lower income groups will be hurt most. Businesses, and thus employment, will be directly affected by cuts in defense and the reduction of subsidies. The effects of the tax increases will also be felt most keenly by private households, but here it is the upper income groups that will suffer most.

The initial bias in the distribution of the financial burden of unification, which assigned a disproportionate share to workers making social security contributions, will be reduced. The effects of Germany's consolidation policies will mostly be felt by neighboring countries.

Policy Options

Three general policy alternatives are available to overcome the difficulties just described. The first relies on quasi-automatic deficit reduction through economic growth. Currently, a 1-percentage-point higher growth rate in *western* Germany provides additional tax receipts of DM 8 billion and additional revenues from social security contributions of DM 6 billion. This amount is rather modest and would contribute in a significant way to deficit reduction only over a number of years. Moreover, a sustained higher growth rate cannot be counted upon. Another source of quasi-automatic deficit reduction, namely, a more rapid adjustment in eastern Germany than currently assumed, would not contribute in a significant way under any realistic scenario. Although the need for housing allowances and social assistance would be reduced, other income-related transfers such as nonwage costs and personnel compensation in the public sector would not decline substantially.

The second strategy relies on discretionary policies. On the revenue side this means first of all the introduction of new taxes. One of the options most often discussed is a tax on carbon dioxide emissions, which at levels currently proposed would generate revenues of DM 9 billion (in 1994) to DM 26 billion (in 2000). Another widely discussed option is to require a labor market contribution by civil servants. Because they do not make unemployment insurance contributions, which are an important source of financing for unification, civil servants do not share the burden of unification equally with employees in the private sector. But subjecting them to unemployment insurance contributions would mean a net deficit reduction of only DM 3 billion annually, not to mention the numerous legal hurdles to be overcome. And while a reduction of tax subsidies for housing may look more promising at first sight (DM 26 billion in potential revenues), the fact that such a measure could not be applied retroactively reduces the potential savings to DM 3 billion annually.

Politically at least, a somewhat more attractive alternative is an increase in tax rates: a 1-percentage-point surcharge on income and corporate taxes generates additional (gross) revenues of DM 4 billion annually, and a 1-percentage-point increase in the value-added tax provides DM 11 billion annually; an increase in the gasoline tax by 10 pfennigs per liter yields DM 5 billion annually. An increase in the wealth tax to levels in effect elsewhere in the European Union would mean additional receipts of DM 15 billion, and if the U.S. standard were adopted these would jump to DM 50 billion. However, such comparisons must keep the completely different tax structures of these countries in mind. More rigorous tax enforcement should also be considered. But although some estimates of revenues lost to tax evasion and abuse run as high as DM 150 billion per year, only about DM 5 billion to DM 10 billion of this could probably be recouped. A still less promising—although widely discussed—approach is the sale of public assets. The annual gross receipts would not exceed DM 1 billion and would be largely offset by current revenues forgone.

On the expenditure side, the discretionary approach could follow the example of "Operation '82" (the ambitious consolidation plan of the early 1980s) with regard to both government consumption and transfers. The potential for further savings, however, is limited, given the cuts already made in conjunction with the federal consolidation program and the savings, consolidation, and growth program of 1993, and given the reduced investment activities of local communities. Moreover, questions about the political feasibility of such a strategy and about its implications for economic growth raise doubts about whether it could be implemented.

Possible areas for cuts include tax-financed transfers to households (housing and child benefits, pensions, and programs that promote saving), which total DM 230 billion, and to businesses (subsidies), which amount to DM 130 billion (both figures are for western Germany only). However, savings from this source are unlikely to exceed 5 percent (DM 10 billion) per year. Better as well as easier prospects for savings lie in the area of non-insurance-related (i.e., redistributive) contributions to social security, which in 1993 amounted to DM 180 billion.

The third strategy relies on structural consolidation. In the present context such a strategy would aim at faster growth and greater productivity increases. This is by far the most ambitious strategy, since all budget categories would be subject to a review based on the criteria of growth and productivity. The analysis should also include non-budget-related aspects such as regulatory policies. The growth effects of such a strategy would of course not be felt for some time. Any such strategy should focus primarily on improving education and research as well as increasing the efficiency of the public sector and lowering the deficit sensitivity of public revenues and expenditures. In conjunction with Germany's ongoing privatization, further reductions in the number of public sector employees combined with a policy of wage restraint could reduce total government expenditures by 2 percent per year. In addition, the government could consider a temporary interruption of the recent income tax cuts, replacing them with a tax policy that allows greater deductions for investment activities.

Policy Recommendations

The federal government's 1994 medium-term fiscal plan, with few exceptions, makes full use of all potential sources on the revenue side. While there may be some room for improvement in its approach (e.g., through reassessment of property values), additional annual revenues therefrom are unlikely to exceed DM 15 billion, or 0.5 percent of total tax revenues. Moreover, any such additional revenues should be used to reduce social security contributions to preunification levels. Another possibility is to reduce taxes, which in 1997 will reach 26 percent of GNP, a level reached only twice before (in 1977 and 1978). Whatever the ultimate use of any additional savings, the government should publicly commit itself to a timely reduction of the level of taxation, in particular by reducing direct taxes. In addition, policymakers should be required to justify any continuation of the solidarity surcharge, which is to be reintroduced in 1995.

The implications of the government's fiscal plan on the expenditure side are equally worrisome, however. As already stated, current planning anticipates government expenditure growth remaining more than 2 percentage points below the growth rate of GNP for the foreseeable future. Previous experience suggests that this is not a very realistic policy scenario, and certainly could not be achieved without impairing economic growth. The consequences for growth would be especially adverse for western Germany, where many expenditure categories would have to experience real, and possibly even nominal, declines, keeping the disproportional needs for transfers to eastern Germany in mind. Besides, it should be clear that, given the magnitude of the contractive macroeconomic effects of deficit reduction, any resulting reduction in interest rates cannot be expected to compensate for or even significantly offset these effects.

It is true that not all expenditure cuts would have a negative impact on economic growth. But when identifying possible areas for further cuts in consumption-type expenditures, it should be remembered that, at least in the early years, the financial burdens of unification were not distributed evenly across all social groups. Additional cuts that are unlikely to affect growth can be made in programs that promote personal saving, construction of housing, and subsidies. These cuts would add up to about DM 3.5 billion to 5 billion, or 0.2 percent of total expenditures. But even considering these additional savings—

most of which would have to be made in western Germany—the reductions in public services planned by the government would almost certainly reduce long-term economic growth. Thus, if the continuation of economic growth and productivity increases requires additional expenditures in such areas as research and development, investment, and education, the government should accept any deficits that arise therefrom. These are unlikely to exceed 0.5 percent of GNP. Moreover, given the pivotal role of western Germany's economy for economic prospects in eastern Germany, additional expenditures here may actually reduce the fiscal dilemma in the medium term.

To justify its deficit reduction plans, which are unusually stringent, in particular by international standards, the government has pointed to the requirements for European Economic and Monetary Union, in particular the Maastricht criteria. However, one should not overlook the central role that the German economy plays in the European economy and in Europe's overall fiscal health as well: a 1-percentage-point increase in Germany's growth rate leads to a 0.2-percentage-point higher growth rate, and an additional DM 6 billion in government revenues, in the European Union as a whole. Moreover, the Maastricht imperatives notwithstanding, there are a number of good reasons to reduce the current level of taxation, for example to improve Germany's competitiveness as well as its institutional framework conditions. The overall goal of domestic growth must also be given much greater consideration when contemplating further expenditure cuts. Such a more balanced perspective will prove more beneficial to Germany, Europe, and the international community than clinging to an arbitrary deficit goal at all costs. Finally, to put the Maastricht criteria into perspective, excluding the Debt Redemption Fund from the calculation reduces Germany's deficit and debt ratios by DM 25 billion (0.7 percentage point) and DM 400 billion (12 percentage points), respectively, freeing an additional DM 25 billion for tax reductions or investments in growth. It should be clear in any case that in the end all these ratios should play only an instrumental role in fiscal policymaking. Meaningful structural consolidation requires a much more ardent and consistent effort, independent of the electoral cycle, on the part of both economic and fiscal policymakers— indeed probably a greater effort than has ever been necessary in the history of the Federal Republic.

I. Wanted: Wirtschaftswunder Number Two?

It is said that there are only two causes for tragedy: not getting what you want, and getting it. Germany may be a case in point. The unification of the two Germanys, finally consummated on October 3, 1990, was something that Germans had sought for forty years. But the elation that Germans felt on that historic date was quickly stilled by rising concerns about the costs of reintegrating two societies whose paths had diverged so sharply during those four decades.

The difficulties encountered in the adjustment process that followed unification have been unexpectedly great, not just in the east but also in the west. Given the somber economic outlook, widespread disenchantment with the political system (*Politikverdrossenheit*), declining voter participation, and escalating right-wing extremist activities, it is hardly surprising that the social and political stability of the Federal Republic has increasingly come into question, especially abroad.[1]

As the eastern part of the German economy continues on its difficult adjustment path, the future costs of unification that Germany and the international community will have to face—especially those stemming from Germany's rising deficit and debt problems—demand attention. Current projections are for the most part pessimistic. But it remains to be seen whether such a dismal view is justified once the facts have been considered rationally and the different dimensions of the problem have been evaluated realistically.

This study tries to answer these questions. It is organized as follows: following this background chapter, chapter 2 examines Germany's macroeconomic and fiscal outlook, in particular the federal government's current medium-term fiscal strategy, and discusses a series of economic and fiscal deficiencies arising from that plan. Based on these findings, chapter 3 examines a broad series of alternative income and expenditure policies aimed at improving the general outlook for fiscal consolidation. The concluding chapter evaluates the government's current fiscal plan, proposes several revisions with respect to both revenue and expenditure planning, and examines the possibilities offered by a less ambitious goal for deficit reduction. Before proceeding with the analysis, however, it is necessary to review briefly the accomplishments of German unification so far, the current estimates of its future costs, and the way in which unification has been financed up to now.

Accomplishments

Evaluations of what has been achieved in the wake of unification four years ago vary according to both the observer and the focus of attention. For example, the initial gap between east and west with regard to transfer income and the structure of consumption—the main source of concern in both parts of Germany—has steadily decreased,[2] but a consideration of the state of the infrastructure and the overall level of economic activity, earned income, and especially employment presents a different picture.

In early 1994, 1.2 million people were registered as unemployed in eastern Germany. That amounts to an unemployment rate of 16.2 percent, and considering the comprehensive labor market measures undertaken in eastern Germany the real rate may even have been 30 percent. In the west, 2.5 million people—9.1 percent of the population—were unemployed, evidence of the fact that western Germany had just gone through one of its worst postwar recessions. The differences in net nominal and real per capita income between east and west decreased to 28 percent and 34 percent, respectively (the corresponding figures for gross per capita income are 30 percent and 38 percent).[3] However, when one looks at these differences in a disaggregated fashion it becomes obvious that the gap between east and west will have to increase for some time because of the fact that wage differentials across regions, sectors, and individuals remain narrower in the east than in the west.

Comparison of the first three years of rapprochement between eastern and western Germany with the transformation process in the countries of Eastern Europe puts the new states (Länder) of Germany in a favorable light. Disposable income in many Eastern European countries has fallen by as much as 50 percent since 1989, huge adjustments in labor markets remain to be made, and inflation is by no means under control.[4] But there is no doubt that even in eastern Germany the economic and human costs of adjustment have been enormous, as indicated by the high rates of official and hidden unemployment.

The Future Costs of Unification

Questions about the future costs and time needed to complete the task of unification are not easily answered, even if one limits the focus to an aggregate view of the economy. Besides the *financial* costs—the transfer payments—the *real* economic costs have to be considered as well: one must examine not only the primary effects of unification, but also the secondary effects due to changes in the behavior of economic actors, with regard to both costs and revenues. Finally, any analysis should focus on net costs and must differentiate between transitory and permanent costs and gains.

Both public discussion and the debate among policymakers and academics in Germany and abroad have ignored such distinctions, focusing instead for the most part on fiscal costs, and in particular the volume of fiscal transfers. The annual transfer of DM 152 billion, or 5 percent of GNP, from west to east between 1991 and 1994 has indeed been a unique event in recent international financial history.[5] According to most estimates, including that of the German federal government, annual transfers as a percentage of GNP will remain about the same until the year 2000.[6]

The current economic situation in western Germany, especially its medium- and long-term prospects, provides ample reason for concern.[7] As will be shown below, this concern is very much supported by empirical evidence, or at least by current projections. But it is also a consequence of the fact that the economic implications of unification were misjudged, not just in the period immediately before and after formal unification but until as recently as 1992. With few exceptions, analysts considered the burdens of financing unification minor and easily manageable.[8] And even though the necessary steps with respect to expenditure, revenue, and credit policy became increasingly obvious, they either were not implemented or were implemented only provisionally.[9] There may have been good reasons for such delay.[10] First, a rough estimate of the financial transfers needed by the new Länder was not available until October 1990, by which time the legal framework of unification had been established. Second, not only were serious mistakes made in evaluating the east's competitiveness, but projections of the east's adjustment needs, its infrastructure needs, the extent to which its public sector would have to be scaled back, and the development of wages proved to be in error. Third, few had predicted the breakdown of the Eastern European and former Soviet markets that had been the destination of so much of eastern Germany's output, or the unusually long global recession of the early 1990s.

It remains a mystery, however, why many observers in Germany expected the realization of potential fiscal savings as well as the reorientation of public expenditures to occur rapidly. Policymakers anticipated savings in 1991 of approximately DM 35 billion as a result of unification. This figure was expected to increase to DM 70 billion by 1994[11] and included an average of DM 11.7 billion per year between 1991 and 1994 from the discontinuation of special subsidies to Berlin and the internal border region, as well as cuts in military expenditures and other potential savings.[12] Moreover, in 1991 medium-term financial planning by the federal government projected annual growth of expenditures in the years 1992 to 1994 at 1.7 percent, or 4 percentage points below nominal GNP growth.[13] As will be shown below, previous experience in the Federal Republic should have lent little credibility to such projections. At least in retrospect, it is hard to understand why the federal government until 1993 categorically ruled out further tax increases (after implementation of the special levy on income and corporate income tax—the so-called solidarity surcharge—for the period July 1, 1991, to June 30, 1992, and the increase of several consumption taxes) and instead counted to a large extent on anticipated cuts in public expenditures.

The Financing of German Unification to Date: Everything Wrong?

Even if these criticisms are valid, one has to consider what would have been the macroeconomic consequences of an alternative policy mix, particularly with regard to the future implications of financing German unification. The transfers made between 1990 and 1994 created an average budget deficit of about 5 percent of GNP, without taking into account the supplementary budgets of the Treuhandanstalt, the Fonds Deutsche Einheit (German Unity Fund), the Kreditabwicklungsfond (Credit Liquidation Fund), and other off-budget entities. Economic stimuli of this magnitude, as well as efforts to neutralize them through tax increases or expenditure cuts, inevitably have considerable macroeconomic repercussions. Econometric simulations indicate that the mix chosen to finance unification for the years 1990 through 1992 was not entirely inappropriate: financing the transfer solely through tax increases or expenditure cuts would have caused either a considerable decline in growth or a sharp increase in inflation;[14] the latter would not have been tolerated by the Bundesbank, whose certain response would have been a monetary tightening that would have decreased growth even more.[15] (The importance of western German growth for the process of reconstruction and revival in the east should not be underestimated, as will be discussed further below.) In addition, there is the commonly held opinion that, in mid-1990, western Germans would have willingly accepted additional tax burdens; this may be intuitively plausible, but historical experience as well as actual evidence suggest the contrary.[16]

The international and especially the Western European community has viewed the financing of unification more critically, for the most part because of its assumed impact on long-term interest rates throughout Europe and beyond.[17] The increase in government-administered prices and social security contributions to finance unification led—along with increased housing rents—to a rise in inflation from less than 2.5 percent prior to unification to an average of 3.5 percent between 1990 and 1993. To counter this development, as well as to prevent an uncontrolled expansion of the federal deficit and debt, the Bundesbank repeatedly increased the discount rate—reducing it, reluctantly, only when the cyclical climate began to worsen in the summer of 1992.

It remains difficult to determine to what degree these policy actions were responsible for the rise in German and international long-term interest rates; after all, these rates tend to be influenced by a multitude of factors. In the Federal Republic, long-term interest rates had already increased by 1 percent in the winter of 1990, at a time when formal unification was still some time off and the future financial burdens for western Germany were still largely unknown.[18] Assuming for the moment that unification did affect interest rates at home and abroad, it is still unclear whether and to what degree this contributed to a deepening of the recession in Europe as well as the United States. In addition, any potential interest rate effects should be balanced against the substantial expansion in trade that resulted from unification. The transfers to eastern Germany in 1990 and 1991 led to increases of 0.5 percent and 0.7 percent, respectively, in real GNP in the countries of the European Union.[19] The corresponding increases for western Germany amounted to 1.5 percent and 2 percent, respectively.[20] There are thus some indications that the net effect of Bundesbank policy on long-term interest rates and on the expansion of trade among Germany's trading partners was initially positive.

Outlook

For 1994 and beyond, the prognosis for the macroeconomic development of the Federal Republic, in particular for western Germany, is less optimistic than it has been during the last five years. One reason is the drastically changed condition of public finances and the consequences thereof for the economy. The fiscal consequences of unification were addressed rather early.[21] However, the recognition that the outlook for growth and employment was modest even without unification, and that under such circumstances the "burden of unity" would be especially heavy, was in general very much underestimated.

It would be wrong to blame either the cyclical difficulties or the increasingly apparent (since 1992) structural difficulties of western Germany solely on unification. At the same time, however, it cannot be denied that the "burden of unity" has reinforced the current economic problems. It has done so directly with regard to, for example, the already high and still-rising burden on the private sector,[22] and indirectly if one acknowledges that any active fiscal policy must be ruled out for the foreseeable future.

Why Deficits May Matter

Since the early 1980s the Federal Republic has almost entirely avoided using active fiscal policy measures to stabilize the economy. It has done so primarily for political reasons, but also because it could afford to do so, thanks to the long period of sustained economic growth during that decade. Unlike many other industrialized nations, the Federal Republic successfully reduced its public sector deficit across almost all budget categories throughout the 1980s. By 1989 this policy had led to a surplus of DM 2.8 billion and permitted tax cuts in 1986, 1988, and 1990 that totaled 2 percent of GNP.

As mentioned above, countercyclical fiscal policy is not on the agenda in the near future either. This time, however, the reason is not a lack of need or of willingness to use it, but the fact that an already high deficit and debt seem to rule it out. Moreover, in 1994 more than 7 percent of federal government expenditures will go toward interest payments, versus only 5.3 percent in 1990. The deteriorating fiscal situation is also reflected in the fact that, in 1993, Germany met the public sector deficit criteria set by the Maastricht agreement on European Monetary Union only with respect to gross debt, and will most likely fail to meet even this criterion in 1995.

A review of possible policy actions to stimulate growth leads to a rather pessimistic outlook, at least for western Germany. For example, increased investment in science and research is, *ceteris paribus*, no longer a possibility. In fact, plans are to cut spending in this area. Much the same can be said for infrastructure investment. Fortunately, neither area is in acute financial need.[23]

Critical questions about the budget deficit and the means available to reduce it must also be raised when the existing burden on private households is considered. Between 1990 and 1994 taxes and social security contributions increased from 40.4 percent to 44.4 percent of GNP; they will probably surpass 46 percent in 1995. Among the countries of the OECD this figure is about average, but among the Group of Seven countries Germany now ranks second (after France). It is true that net real per capita income in 1993 was in line with the trend from 1960 to 1989. But in 1995 the growth rate of net personal income is likely to fall again—as it did in 1991 and 1992—as a result of the fiscal policy measures mentioned above. This decline is partly due to the fact that until 1993 about 25 percent of the costs of unification were financed by an increase in social security contributions,[24] with the consequence that the 75 percent of persons with earned income who are liable to social security contributions were especially hard hit, while others such as civil servants (12 percent of income earners) and the self-employed (13 percent)[25] had to contribute only modestly to unification. Moreover, a number of income categories (such as capital gains) were exempted entirely.

The developments sketched out above not only have reinforced the rather pessimistic medium-term outlook for the German economy but have even raised doubts about Germany's ability to overcome its immediate cyclical difficulties. However, as already indicated, this line of argument is not entirely legitimate, because the roots of the Federal Republic's slow growth and subsequent employment problems can be traced further back (figure 1-1). During the deficit-financed unification boom these problems were at best covered up, and soon resurfaced.

Some may seek to dismiss this pessimistic prognosis by pointing to economists' rather modest record of success in predicting long- and medium-term economic conditions. From a policymaking perspective, however, this is neither an adequate nor a reasonable answer. And while it is true that the public sector deficit and the overall debt do little to immediately justify the pessimism regarding growth in the Federal Republic, they do deserve to be taken seriously for several other reasons, in particular because of their possible effects on economic growth.

In principle there are three mechanisms by which the deficit can be linked to the level of real interest rates and therefore to economic growth: the first linkage is through the country's rates of saving, investment, and capital accumulation—in other words, the question of how national savings can be used most efficiently; the second is through the policy mix, or to what extent a credible policy of deficit reduction is supported by an accommodating monetary policy, and consequently by lower long-term real interest rates; the third is through the risk of inflation, which may have a disproportionate effect on nominal interest rates. To the extent that credible deficit reduction is accompanied by reduced inflationary expectations, this also leads to lower real interest

Figure 1-1. Key Indicators of the West German Economy, 1950–1993

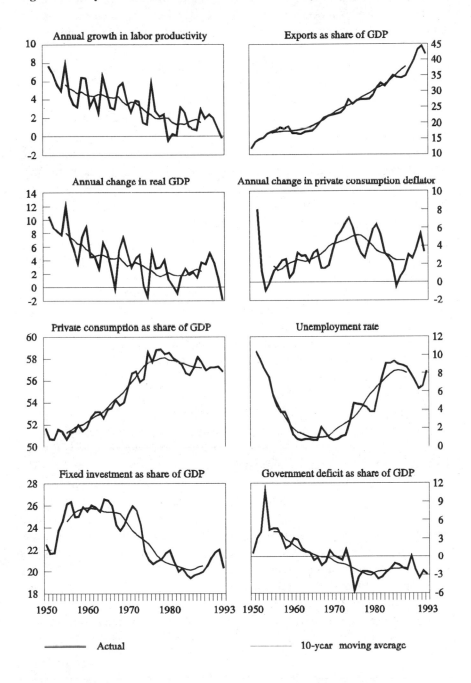

rates.[26] As will be shown below, the empirical validity and relevance of these mechanisms vary widely.[27] But as far as the causal link between public sector deficits and real interest rates is concerned, the Federal Republic is no exception to the general principle.

More recently the relationship between investment and saving has also been discussed in an international context.[28] Here the main issues are to what extent *domestic* investment is determined or limited by *domestic* saving, and whether capital flows have become sufficiently mobile internationally to align interest rates in domestic capital markets. The empirical evidence is not unambiguous. For example, in a recent comprehensive study, Barry Bosworth concluded that national barriers still limit the international mobility of capital, and thus that domestic saving and domestic investment still must balance. Reducing the public sector deficit and therefore its absorption of domestic saving thus has direct implications for the level of domestic investment.[29]

There are thus a number of good reasons to analyze the public finances of the Federal Republic and the budgetary consequences of German unification, all pointing to its implications for saving and investment and thus ultimately economic growth. No comprehensive and concrete analysis of the German economy and its outlook from this perspective has yet been done.[30] Does the Federal Republic really need a "second Wirtschaftswunder," as an American observer noted,[31] or are the fiscal policies implemented to date sufficient to cope with the difficulties? The question is too complex to allow a short, simple answer. First, there are the basic public policy aspects (*Ordnungspolitik*) of the public sector share of GNP, tax rates, and public sector deficits, all of which have reached historically high levels for Germany. Second, there is the question of improving growth and productivity and managing the unemployment problem. Third, there is the danger of displacement or plateau effects, that is, the concern that if the public sector share of the economy remains too high for too long it will be difficult to restore it to its former level. Besides this quantitative displacement there is also the danger of a qualitative displacement, considering the growth and structural policies in the new Länder. As already noted, the analysis that follows is limited to the first aspect of the problem, even though Germany's macroeconomic performance is in some sense a central determinant (and perhaps even a solution) of the fiscal problems. But there are hardly any solutions to this problem in sight, and certainly no new ones, and their discussion goes well beyond the scope of the present study. The same holds true for the constitutional and judicial questions surrounding unification.[32]

II. Macroeconomic and Fiscal Outlook

A country's fiscal outlook is determined by the underlying fiscal conditions at the time of the assessment and by policymakers' decisions about future revenues and expenditures, as well as by overall macroeconomic developments. Both aspects must be examined simultaneously to arrive at an appraisal of future incomes and expenditures that is realistic as well as politically sustainable. In the case of German unification, such an analysis is made more difficult by several factors. For example, the relationship between the government's revenue-expenditure balance and the country's macroeconomic development—beyond the national account effects, as in the case of earned income and taxation[1]—is known only with respect to its direction; the strength and the time profile of this relationship vary, and efforts to estimate them have not produced very accurate results. With the Federal Republic about to reach levels of taxation (especially of households) for which there is no historical precedent, accurate estimates will be especially difficult. Although there are examples in the history of public finance where quantum leaps of this kind, in either direction, did not have the effects anticipated or feared,[2] and indeed some of Germany's neighbors have found themselves in similar situations, certain risks do exist and cannot be excluded a priori.

The analysis here is limited to the income-expenditure relationship between the fiscal system and the economy as described by macroeconometric models.[3] Following the routine practice of the German authorities, these effects will be presented in gross terms, although with taxes and other levies amounting to more than 45 percent of GNP this will not yield an accurate picture. For example, in the case of increases in expenditures or revenues, the net effects on the deficit (based on three-year averages) only amount to about 60 percent of the gross effects.[4]

Macroeconomic Conditions from 1993 to 1997

By early 1994 western Germany had begun to recover from one of its worst postwar recessions.[5] The pace of recovery, however, is expected to be slow, with real GDP growth in 1994 between 0.5 and 1.0 percent, as it has been in recent years in the United States, Canada, and the United Kingdom. Sluggish growth together with productivity gains and a growing labor force is expected to lead to a further increase in unemployment by about 400,000 people in 1994, creating a record-high unemployment rate of 9.5 percent.

As so often is the case in such situations, the medium-term outlook for the Federal Republic is also grim. This has once again led to a debate about Germany's competitiveness, in which concern about *"Standort Deutschland"* (Germany's competitive position) figures prominently.[6] Given these economic prospects, as well as an excess supply of labor for the foreseeable future, medium-term projections are especially problematic, since they traditionally disregard any capacity problems by assuming full capacity utilization.[7] The notion that western Germany will soon recoup the ground lost in the recession and return to a growth path of 2.0 to 2.5 percent of real GDP (comparable to that achieved between 1980 and 1990, when the average was 2.1 percent) is rather unlikely at this point; and even this modest success would mean an unemployment rate still above 6 percent. In any case, assuming a steady increase in the rate of productivity, growth within this range would contribute little to reducing the previously accumulated level of unemployment.

Economic development in eastern Germany is even harder to predict. Estimates of the duration of the adjustment process for eastern and western Germany vary between 5 and 35 years (although not all the authors of these forecasts define "adjustment" in the same way).[8]

This skeptical view of Germany's economic outlook is reinforced by difficulties in the international economic environment. The long and difficult transformation process in Eastern Europe, open as well as hidden problems in the Triad, and difficulties in the European Union's internal and external relations likewise do not yield a very positive scenario for the international—and hence for the German—economy.[9]

The above scenarios illustrate a further difficulty: many of these problems are unprecedented in their structure and intensity. Basically all of the G-7 countries are currently confronted with similar economic difficulties: high government deficits, increasing government debts, slow growth, and rising structural unemployment. It is difficult to foresee how economic policy can and will react to these challenges.[10]

In light of these new and complicating factors, any prognosis has to be fashioned with much caution. Current forecasts of real GDP growth in Germany for 1992 to 1997 vary between 1.5 percent (the federal government's estimate)[11] and 2.5 percent per year.[12] The government's projection[13] implies no reduction in the 1993 unemployment rate of 7.3 percent. The more optimistic forecast predicts a decline in unemployment by 1997 to its 1992 level of 5.8 percent. The analysis here is primarily based on the more optimistic of the two prognoses, and this should be kept in mind in the discussion of the policy implications. However, for comparative purposes we will also refer from time to time to the federal government's economic scenario.

Assumptions

Before exploring the forecasts in greater detail, it is necessary to discuss briefly some of the underlying assumptions. This not only allows for a better understanding of the general demographic and economic policy conditions in (western) Germany but is also of importance in evaluating the various consolidation strategies presented later. The assumptions themselves are not likely to be very controversial. Disagreements are likely to center mainly around the actions that might be taken by the government (e.g., the number of public sector employees, the level of social security contributions) and are not of central importance for the overall economic picture. The most important assumptions underlying the medium-term economic outlook forecast are summarized below (table 2-1).

According to the most recent study by the Federal Statistical Office (Statistisches Bundesamt), the decline in the *population* of western Germany has come to an end. However, this turnaround is not due to an increase in birth rates, but to the rising influx of immigrants and of ethnic Germans formerly living abroad. The number of foreigners residing in western Germany is still rising, although at a slower rate. By 1997 their number is expected to rise to 6.5 million—an increase of 0.6 million from 1992, but a relatively small increment compared with the increase from 4.8 million to 5.7 million between 1988 and 1991. The number of German nationals is expected to rise by about 1.2 million between 1992 and 1997.

The *labor market participation rate* of Germans as well as of resident foreigners is expected to decrease slightly, assuming a slower rate of immigration of families. As a result, the number of employed persons will rise at a slower rate than the resident population; the fact that 300,000 people commute to Germany for work amplifies the slow rate of growth. Overall, the number of wage earners will increase by 1 percent.

Labor productivity is assumed to increase by 1.5 percent annually—the same as between 1990 and 1992. Given a further reduction in working hours of

Table 2-1. Assumptions Underlying the Medium-Term Forecast for the Western German Economy, 1980-1997
Percentages except where stated otherwise

	1980	1990	1991	1992[a]	1993-97
Population (millions)					
All residents	61.5	63.7	64.1	64.9	66.7[b]
Foreigners	4.5	5.3	5.7	5.9	6.5[b]
Nationals	57.0	58.5	58.4	59.0	60.2[b]
Labor market participation rates					
Foreigners	54.8	56.0	56.0	56.0	56.0
Nationals	45.9	49.4	49.7	49.6	49.7
Productivity and employment (percentage changes)					
Output per wage earner	2.5[c]	1.2[d]	1.5	1.5	1.5
Hours worked per wage earner	0.8	-0.6[d]	-1.0	-1.0	-1.0
Domestic labor force	0.2	0.5[d]	2.6	1.0	1.0
Public sector employment	2.9	0.9[d]	0.5	0.5	-0.5
Transborder commuters	-0.1[c]	0.0[d]	0.2	0.3	0.3
World economy					
Growth in world trade	5.6[c]	4.8[d]	3.0	6.0	6.0
Exchange rate (DM per dollar)	1.8	1.6	1.7	1.7	1.7
Oil price (dollars per barrel)	34.4	23.6	19.1	20.4	24.2
Taxes and social security contributions					
Value added tax	13.0	14.0	14.0	14.0	15.0
Corporate income tax	56.0	50.0	50.0	50.0	45.0
Social security contributions					
Unemployment insurance	3.0	4.3	6.8	6.3	5.7
Health insurance	11.4	12.5	12.2	12.7	13.1[e]
Pension insurance	18.0	18.7	17.7	17.7	18.2
Investment and interest rates					
Increase in public sector gross fixed investment					
in construction	5.0[c]	0.0[d]	6.0	5.0	4.0
Long-term real estate	3.4	5.5	4.8	4.5	4.5

Source: Official data; authors' calculations and estimates.

a. Partially estimated for 1993
b. Figures are for 1997
c. Average annual change, 1970–1980.
d. Average annual change, 1980–1990.
e. Excludes long-term care insurance.

1 percent per year, hourly productivity is expected to increase by 2.5 percent per year.

The volume of *world trade* is expected to grow by an average of 6 percent annually in real terms. This is based on the assumption that the world economy will regain momentum after its sluggish performance between 1990 and 1992. In addition, it is expected that the western German economy will profit from continued strong demand from the new Länder, at least until the mid-1990s.[14] The exchange rate between the deutsche mark and the U.S. dollar is projected to be DM 1.70. Further real devaluations or revaluations within the EMS (European Monetary System) are not assumed. The price of crude oil will further increase in nominal terms but will stay almost constant in real terms.

The value-added tax (VAT) rate is assumed to remain at 15 percent during the forecast period. Social security contributions will continue to rise: unemployment insurance to 5.7 percent, health insurance to 13.1 percent, and retirement insurance to 18.2 percent of income liable to contributions.[15] Gross investment in construction by the federal government will grow by only 4 percent per year in nominal terms, after almost 7 percent per year in 1989 and 1990. The number of federal employees will rise only marginally. Generally speaking, this forecast assumes a dampening impact of the federal government on overall economic development—not surprising considering the very tight budgetary conditions. Fortunately, given the high quality and durability of existing infrastructure, no significant infrastructure deficit is expected.

With respect to *monetary developments*, long-term real interest rates are assumed to remain constant. However, the present level of about 4.5 percent is comparatively high in the experience of the Federal Republic. (The real interest rate between 1961 and 1975 was also 4.5 percent, but overall economic growth during that period was much stronger.) Between 1971 and 1980 and between 1981 and 1990 the rates were 2.9 percent and 6.3 percent, respectively.

With respect to *environmental policy*, the forecast assumes the status quo: all prospective measures to protect the environment and all current legislation and administrative rulings that have not yet been implemented are excluded.[16]

A few additional assumptions (e.g., regarding wage policy) will be discussed when examining the implications of the forecast.

Macroeconomic Projections

WESTERN GERMANY. Based on the set of assumptions just presented and on the hypotheses underlying the model used here,[17] real western German GNP is

Table 2-2. Macroeconomic Trends in Western Germany, 1980-1997

	1980	1990	1991	1992	1993	1997
Employment (thousands)						
Resident wage earners	27,059	28,486	28,993	29,141	28,652	...
Transborder commuters[a]	-79	-7	234	346	362	...
Domestic wage earners	26,980	28,479	29,227	29,487	29,014	31,000
Unemployed	889	1,883	1,689	1,808	2,270	...
Demand components (percentages of GDP)						
Private consumption	55.3	54.3	54.2	54.3	55.3	54.5
Public consumption	20.4	18.5	17.7	18.0	18.1	16.8
Gross fixed investment	22.6	21.1	21.4	21.4	20.3	21.1
Machinery and equipment	8.5	9.6	10.0	9.4	8.2	9.9
Construction	14.1	11.6	11.5	11.9	12.1	11.2
Additions to inventories	0.6	0.7	0.3	-0.1	-0.8	0.0
Net exports	1.1	5.5	6.4	6.5	7.2	7.6
Exports	23.6	31.1	33.9	34.6	33.1	38.5
Imports	22.5	25.6	27.5	28.1	26.9	30.8
Real GDP (millions of DM)	2,018.0	2,520.4	2,635.0	2,676.0	2,622.5	3,042.0
General government (billions of DM)						
Receipts	669.0	1,051.7	1,170.1	1,277.3	1,309.5	1,524.0
Expenditures	711.7	1,101.5	1,272.4	1,341.0	1,389.0	1,624.0
Balance	-42.7	-49.7	-102.2	-63.8	-79.5	-100.0

expected to grow by 2.6 percent per year between 1992 and 1997 (table 2-2). Most of this growth will be sustained by private consumption, much as in the equally sluggish 1970s. Public consumption will increase only slightly. Given the expansions in training, education, and health care since the 1970s, this modest increase will not create any major bottlenecks. Investment will increase only modestly; given current capital-output ratios, investment will not expand sufficiently to satisfy the growth or productivity requirements.

Growth in Germany's foreign trade is expected to remain consistently above the historical average during the period, although export growth will be below that of world trade. By 1997 exports should account for 38.5 percent of GNP. (Government transfers to eastern Germany are still by convention treated as exports.) Net exports will increase to 7.6 percent of GNP. The inflation rate as measured by the consumer price index will average 2.3 percent per year. A

Table 2-2. (cont.) Macroeconomic Trends in Western Germany, 1980–1997

	1980–1990	1991	1992	1993	1994–1997
	Average annual percentage changes				
Employment					
Resident wage earners	0.5	1.8	0.5	-1.7	...
Transborder commuters	...	...	...	...	...
Domestic wage earners	0.5	2.6	0.9	-1.6	1.0
Unemployed	...	...	...	...	...
Demand components					
Private consumption	2.1	4.5	1.7	0.0	2.7
Public consumption	1.2	0.3	3.2	-1.3	1.2
Gross fixed investment	1.8	6.1	1.1	-6.9	2.2
Machinery and equipment	3.5	9.1	-3.9	-15.0	3.6
Construction	0.3	3.6	5.5	-0.5	1.3
Additions to inventories	...	...	...	...	...
Net exports	...	...	...	...	...
Exports	5.1	13.7	3.7	-6.1	4.8
Imports	3.6	12.1	3.9	-9.5	4.5
Gross national product	2.2	4.5	1.6	-1.9	2.6
Prices					
Private consumption deflator	2.5	3.7	4.0	3.4	2.3
GDP deflator	2.8	3.9	4.4	3.3	2.5
General government					
Receipts	4.6	12.2	8.2	2.5	3.6
Expenditures	4.5	15.5	5.4	3.6	3.9
Balance	...	...	...	...	...

Source: Federal Statistical Office and authors' calculations and estimates.

a. Negative numbers indicate more German residents commuting to work outside Germany than non-German residents commuting to Germany.

decline in unemployment is unlikely. Government expenditures will lag behind revenues—this is largely a politically driven development and will lead to a reduction of the deficit as a percentage of GNP. Considering that government interest payments will be growing at a much faster than average rate, the annual increase in the remaining expenditures is not likely to exceed 2 percent—a decline in real terms.

As indicated above, the underlying assumptions lend themselves to different forecasts. The differences between the two forecasts presented here lie within the typical range for this type of forecast.[18] In this particular case, changes in the GNP/GDP deflator will narrow the differences with respect to growth of nominal GDP, which is expected to be 2.3 percent, while the federal government expects an inflation rate of 3.0 percent. Regarding nominal GNP/GDP, which is the central determinant on the revenue side of the federal budget, the difference between growth rates decreases to 0.5 percentage point.

Assuming that the incomes of wage earners stay in line with productivity—which, given the labor market situation, is by no means certain—gross per capita income should increase by about 1.5 percent per year. However, considering the planned increase in taxes and social security contributions, stagnation of net income per capita cannot be ruled out.

EASTERN GERMANY Eastern Germany's macroeconomic development is of interest here, despite the forecasting problems described earlier, only because it is the principal determinant of the future transfer needs of the new Länder. The structural composition of eastern German growth, its level, and so on, are ignored.

The federal government has issued the following forecasts for eastern Germany (table 2-3):[19] first, GDP per wage earner (i.e., productivity) in 1997 will amount to DM 50,000, or 55 percent of that in the west; second, the most important determinant of growth on the demand side, namely, investment in plant and equipment, will grow in real terms at an average annual rate of 12 percent, and in nominal terms at 17 percent; third, the new Länder will continue to generate considerable demand for transfers. Despite growing exports (not shown here), the negative external balance of the new Länder will increase from DM 196 billion to DM 239 billion between 1992 and 1997.

Only the federal government has published estimates of future transfer requirements to the east (table 2-4): about 5 percent of GNP annually.[20] Assuming that GNP is DM 3.8 trillion in 1997, gross transfer payments would then amount to DM 190 billion. ("Gross" here means excluding any increase in revenues from taxes and other contributions resulting from these transfers,

Table 2-3. Macroeconomic Trends in Eastern Germany, Actual and Projected, 1991–1997

Billions of DM, except where stated otherwise

	1991	1992	1997	1992–97[a]
Labor force (thousands) of which:	6,344	6,344	6,200	0.5
Dependent employment	5,933	5,933	5,500	-1.0
GDP (at 1991 prices)	180.9	198.4	273.0	6.5
GDP per wage earner[b]	-11.4	26.8	...	7.0
GDP deflator[b]	15.9	17.6	...	6.0
GDP (at current prices)	180.9	233.4	431.0	13.0
Private consumption	179.4	212.0	105.9	7.5
Public consumption	85.6	105.8	125.0	3.5
Gross fixed investment	87.2	115.6	237.0	17.0
Net exports	-171.4	-197.6	-239.0	...

Source: Bundesministerium der Finanzen, *Finanzbericht 1994* (Bonn, 1993), pp.71ff., and Federal Statistical Office.

a. Average annual rate of change.
b. Percentage change from previous year.

as well as the savings, mentioned previously, realized from the disarmament of and subsidies to the internal border region and Berlin; these amounted to about DM 54 billion, or one-third of the gross transfer by the government in 1993.[21]) According to the Ministry of Finance, the federal government would cover about two-thirds of the gross transfer, including subsidies to the Federal Employment Agency. The amount would be distributed among the state and local budgets, contributions to individuals, and other agencies of the federal government, with each receiving one-third of the total.[22]

Table 2-4. Western German Fiscal Transfers to Eastern Germany, Actual and Projected, 1991–1997

Billions of DM

	1991	1992	1993	1994[a]	1995	1996	1997
Financial transfers to territorial authorities[b]	107.0	115.2	116.5	120.1	156.4	164.0	170.0
German Unity Fund	35.0	36.1	36.4	34.6	...	...	...
Unification-related expenditures of federal government (settlement of balances)[c]	59.2	65.1	65.7	70.0	103.4	107.5	110.5
Debt Redemption Fund	...	...	...	...	29.8	30.0	30.0
Equalization of turnover tax by Länder	10.8	11.5	11.4	12.5	...	...	...
Restructuring of the revenue equalization scheme	...	...	...	...	50.0	53.0	56.0
Transfers by Länder	2.0	2.5	3.0	3.0	3.0	3.5	3.5
Transfers to social security insurance	21.4	40.4	43.0	41.0	39.0	37.0	35.0
Unemployment insurance	21.4	35.4	35.0	31.0	29.0	...	...
Pension insurance	...	5.0	8.0	10.0	10.0	...	...
All transfers	128.4	155.6	163.5	161.1	195.4	201.0	205.0
Memorandum: Borrowing by the Treuhandanstalt	19.9	29.6	38.1	44.0	...	...	...

Source: *Die Lage der Weltwirtschaft und der deutschen Wirtschaft im Früjahr 1994,* an evaluation of the German economic situation conducted by the following members of the Arbeitsgemeinschaft deutscher wirtschaftswissenschaftlicher Forschungsinstitute e.V., Munich; Deutsches Institut füf Wirtschaftsforschung Berlin; HWWA-Institut für Wirtschaftsforschung Hamburg; ifo Institut für Wirtschaftsforschung, Munich; Institut für Weltwirtschaft Universität Kiel; Institut für Wirtschaftsforschung Halle; Rheinisch-Westfälisches Institut für Wirtschaftsforschung, Essen; p.20 (table), and authors' calculations.

a. Estimates of participating institutes
b. Excludes interest subsides for ERP credits.
c. Excludes revenue losses due to investment support in the new Länder, and excludes borrowing by the Treuhandanstalt.

Implications of the projections

What are the implications of the economic forecast just described? Consistent with the focus of this study, we address the implications for the public sector and private households first, then the consequences for the business sector, and finally, any potential repercussions for the international community.

THE DEFICIT. The recent trend in the public sector deficit is depicted in tables 2-5 and 2-6. The deficits of local communities have experienced, in relative terms, the sharpest increase, although this was from low initial levels. The federal deficit has increased little in percentage terms compared with that of the local governments—a fact that can be explained by the rising importance of supplementary budgets since unification. Here the Treuhandanstalt, the institution charged with the privatization of eastern German state enterprises, ranks first, with net borrowing of DM 38.1 billion in 1993, followed by the German Unity Fund.[23] The deficits of the Bundesbahn and the Reichsbahn (DM 8.5 billion), the Bundespost (DM 8 billion), and the federal financing institutions have also increased severalfold. Taken together, the deficits of all public institutions at the national level amounted to almost DM 220 billion in 1993.[24]

According to the 1993 medium-term fiscal planning of the federal, state, and local governments, the territorial authorities' combined deficit will be reduced from almost DM 160 billion (DM 114 billion in national account terms) in 1993 to DM 60 billion in 1997.[25] Assuming nominal GNP in western Germany of DM 3.4 trillion in 1997, or 5 percent nominal growth compared with 1992, this implies a deficit share of GNP of 1.8 percent. This share would be below the norm established by the German Council of Economic Experts in the 1980s (2 percent of GNP).[26]

THE DEBT. The total debt, according to this forecast, would increase to DM 1.6 trillion by the end of 1997, compared with DM 1.5 trillion at the end of 1993 and 1.3 trillion in 1992. If supplementary budgets and additional expenses are included, the 1997 figure rises to DM 2.2 trillion. As with the deficit, local government will experience the sharpest percentage increase in debt.

The supplementary budgets will be restructured by subsuming the Credit Liquidation Fund and the debts of the Treuhandanstalt into the Debt Redemption Fund (*Erblastentilgungsfond*). Overall, these budgets are expected to increase to about DM 400 billion.[27] The transfer of the Treuhandanstalt's debt will lead to a considerable reduction of the supplementary budgets. The debts of the eastern and western German railways will be consolidated into a

Table 2-5. Public Sector Finances, Actual and Projected, 1950–1997

Percentages of GNP

Year	Expenditures[a]	Taxes[a]	Social Security contribution receipts[a]	Other receipts[a]	Budget balances[a]	Indebtedness[b]
			Preunification Federal Republic			
1950	31.1	21.0	8.5	2.3	0.6	21.0
1960	32.9	23.0	10.3	2.6	3.0	17.4
1970	39.1	24.0	12.6	2.7	0.2	18.6
1980	48.9	25.8	16.8	3.4	-2.9	31.7
1981	49.7	25.1	17.4	3.6	-3.7	35.4
1982	50.0	24.8	17.9	4.0	-3.3	38.7
1983	48.7	24.8	17.3	4.1	-2.5	40.1
1984	48.1	24.9	17.3	4.0	-1.9	40.7
1985	47.7	25.1	17.4	4.1	-1.1	41.4
1986	47.1	24.4	17.4	4.0	-1.3	41.4
1987	47.4	24.5	17.5	3.5	-1.9	42.4
1988	47.0	24.3	17.4	3.2	-2.1	42.8
1989	45.3	24.9	17.0	3.5	0.1	41.3
1990	45.8	23.5	16.8	3.5	-2.0	43.2
			Unified Federal Republic			
1991	49.1	24.3	18.0	3.6	-3.2	41.3
1992	49.8	24.8	18.4	4.0	-2.6	44.2
1993	51.2	24.8	19.1	3.9	-3.3	48.4
			Forecast			
1994	51.6	25.0	19.5	4.0	-3.1	54.0
1995	51.2	25.7	19.6	3.7	-2.8	62.5
1996	51.0	25.9	19.4	3.7	-2.0	62.0
1997	50.0	26.0	19.1	3.6	-1.4	60.0

Source: *Die Lage der Weltwirtschaft und der deutschen Wirtschaft im Früjahr 1994* (see table 2-4), Federal Statistical Office, Deutsche Bundesbank, and authors' calculations.

a. National account basis, which includes all territorial authorities and social security insurance, but not the Treuhandanstalt.
b. Public sector budgets (excluding social security insurance); beginning with 1995 includes debt of the Treuhandanstalt and public housing of the former Eastern Germany; figures as of year's end.

Table 2-6. Indebtedness of Public Authorities, Actual and Projected, 1989–1997

Borrower	1989	1990	1991	1992	1993	1997
Territorial authorities						
Net market borrowing	25.8	112.2	106.8	120.4	160.0	...
Indebtedness at year's end	928.8	...	...	1,345.2	1,507.8	2,161.0
General Budgets						
Net market borrowing	24.8	75.0	69.4	71.4	71.0	...
Financial balance	-20.9	-71.6	-87.0	-87.9	-134.4	...
Indebtedness at year's end	921.8	...	...	1.154.8	1,290.6	1,641.0
Federal government						
Net market borrowing	15.4	51.6	30.2	20.3	78.5	...
Financial balance	-20.0	-48.0	-53.2	-39.3	-66.9	...
Indebtedness at year's end	490.5	...	...	611.1	685.3	888.0
State governments						
Net market borrowing	7.3	19.2	24.1	36.8	45.5	...
Financial balance	-2.6	-19.4	-29.8	-31.5	-46.5	...
Indebtedness at year's end	309.9	...	...	389.1	434.0	512.0
Local governments[a]						
Net market borrowing	2.1	4.2	15.1	16.4	18.5	...
Financial balance	1.7	-4.2	-4.0	-17.1	-21.0	...
Indebtedness at year's end	121.4	...	...	154.6	171.3	241.0
Supplementary budgets						
ERP Fund						
Financial balance	1.1	2.4	6.9	7.9	4.0	...
Indebtedness at year's end	7.1	...	...	24.3	28.3	50.0
German Unity Fund						
Financial balance	...	19.8	30.7	23.9	13.5	...
Indebtedness at year's end	...	...	...	74.4	87.7	...
Credit Liquidation Fund						
Financial balance	...	14.9	-0.2	-0.3	0.0	...
Indebtedness at year's end	...	...	...	91.7	101.2	...
Debt Redemption Fund						
Indebtedness at year's end	...	...	...	...	...	400.0

Table 2-6 (cont.)Indebtedness of Public Authorities, Actual and Projected, 1989–1997

Borrower	1989	1990	1991	1992	1993	1997
Federal railway assets						
Indebtedness at year's end	...	...	...	...	...	70.0
Totals for supplementary budgets						
Financial balance	1.1	37.1	37.4	31.5	17.5	...
Indebtedness at year's end	7.1	...	...	190.4	217.2	520.0
Other public authorities						
*Treuhandanstalt*c						
Financial balance	...	4.3	19.9	28.9	39.0	...
Indebtedness at year's end	...	...	...	106.8	168.3	...
Railways						
Financial balance	1.3	4.4	7.3	13.4	12.5	...
Indebtedness at year's end	44.1	...	...	56.5	71.0	...
Post Office						
Financial balance	2.0	4.8	10.3	15.4	8.0	...
Indebtedness at year's end	66.2	...	...	96.6	104.5	...
Development banks						
Financial balance	12.4	16.3	30.0	27.3	...	...
Totals for other public authorities						
Financial balance	15.7	29.8	67.5	85.0	...	...

Source: Deutsche Bundesbank. Bundesministerium der Finanzen, state governments, and authors' calculations and estimates.

a. Includes specific purpose associations.
b. Newly accumulated debt of the East German budget between 1 July 1990 and 2 October 1990, which was assumed by the Credit Liquidation Fund on 3 October 1990 as part of Germany's overall debt.
c. After deduction of redemptions of old debt.

special fund, the *Sondervermögen*, and are to be amortized out of the federal budget over the next three decades.

Given their limited ability to incur debt, the prospects for the social security insurance funds appear more favorable. The pension and health care insurance funds will have balanced budgets by 1997, while the budget of the Federal Employment Agency (Bundesanstalt für Arbeit) should have a deficit of between DM 20 billion and DM 30 billion. This assumes that contributions for unemployment insurance are not raised again. To balance this agency's budget, contribution rates would have to be raised by about 2 percentage points.

Inserting these numbers into the expected economic scenario reveals the following picture: The deficit-GNP ratio will decrease from about 5 percent in 1993 to about 1.8 percent in 1997; meanwhile the federal debt will drop from 44 percent to 42 percent of GNP. If one includes the supplementary budgets, the debt-GNP ratio rises from 51 percent to 56 percent. The federal share of the debt will rise from 20 percent to 22 percent of GNP, that of the Länder will remain at about 13 percent, and the debt of local governments will increase considerably, from 5.1 percent to 6.2 percent. However, it is important to keep in mind that the federal government will absorb the interest and amortization charges as part of the consolidation of the supplementary and other budget categories into the Debt Redemption Fund.[28] The expected amortizations of this fund and the German Unity Fund will not change this picture decisively by the end of this decade.

It is true that indicators such as the deficit-GNP ratio have been criticized for being too mechanical.[29] In this context it should be noted that the calculations here do not include potential secondary effects of expenditure cuts or revenue increases in the public sector on growth and the future fiscal capacity of the economy. Whether any projected cuts in expenditures will be neutralized by declining long-term interest rates is equally questionable, however (see below).

Nevertheless, a comparison with the 1940s and the early 1950s shows that conditions after World War II were incomparably better (figure 2-1). The monetary reform of 1948 canceled all public debts, and the new debt accumulated at a slow pace until the early 1960s.[30] Until 1965 the deficit and debt ratios never surpassed 2 percent and 20 percent, respectively. The circumstances were also more favorable in a political sense, in that the Allied Control Council had made the sensitive decisions regarding burden sharing accompanying monetary reform.[31] It thus freed the first postwar German government from this political minefield.[32]

One can go still further back in history in search of precedents. In 1871 the German Empire also started with a debt ratio of zero, thanks to its ability to use French war reparation payments to settle the outstanding debt of the empire's predecessor, the Northern German Federation.[33]

Taking a more contemporary perspective, and comparing Germany's fiscal condition with that of other countries, reveals a more favorable picture (table 2-7). Among the more important industrial economies in the Organization for

Figure 2-1. Composition of Public Sector Debt and Debt-GNP Ratio, 1950–1993

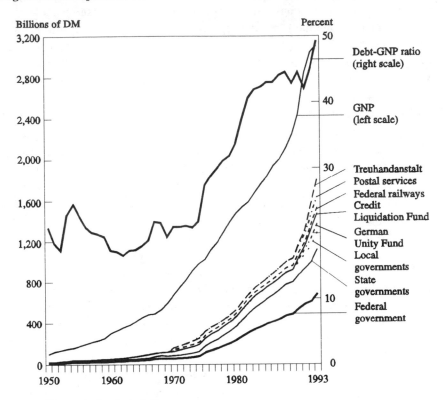

Source: Authors' calculations.

Economic Cooperation and Development (OECD), only Japan, Austria, and Switzerland had lower deficit-GNP ratios than Germany in 1993.[34] In terms of the overall debt-GNP ratio, the United Kingdom and France were in a more favorable position than Germany, whereas the ratios in Japan (68 percent) and the United States (63 percent) were considerably higher (figures 2-2 and 2-3).[35] The majority of the G-7 countries have announced deficit reduction measures similar to Germany's over the coming years. The United States, for example, intends to decrease the federal budget deficit from 4 percent of GDP in fiscal year 1993 to 2.3 percent in fiscal year 1997.[36] Under current plans, the German deficit-GNP ratio is likely to maintain its relatively favorable (by international standards) position until 1997. As to the overall debt ratio, the Federal Republic is likely to drop to the middle of the OECD ranks by 1995, primari-

Table 2-7. Public Sector Deficit Ratios in Selected OECD Countries, 1992 and 1993

Percentages of GDP

Country	Public sector balance		Gross public sector debt	
	1992	1993	1992	1993
Belgium	-6.9	-7.4	131.9	138.4
Canada	-6.6	-7.0	83.3	88.3
Denmark	-2.6	-4.4	73.4	78.5
France	-3.9	-5.9	39.2	44.9
Germany	-2.6	-3.4	44.6	48.0
Greece	-13.2	-15.4	106.7	113.6
Ireland	-2.2	-3.0	91.6	92.9
Italy	-9.5	-10.0	108.0	115.8
Japan	2.6	1.0	67.3	68.3
Luxembourg	-2.5	-2.5	7.3	10.0
Netherlands	-3.5	-4.0	79.7	83.1
Portugal	-5.2	-8.9	63.5	69.5
Spain	-4.6	-7.2	48.8	55.6
United Kingdom	-5.9	-7.6	47.3	53.2
United States[b]	-4.5	-3.6	61.7	63.4
Memorandum: Maastricht criteria	-3	-3	60	60

Source: Deutsche Bundesbank, European Commission, country submissions.

a. National account basis (including social security insurance, not including public enterprises) at the year's end.
b. Excludes liabilities of the deposit insurance system.

ly because of the inclusion of the supplementary budgets. As far as the Maastricht Treaty commitments are concerned, the Federal Republic may fail to meet both the deficit and the debt criterion during 1994 and 1995.

DEBT STRUCTURE. In the United States it has become increasingly conventional to distinguish between the *internal* and the *external* debt. Since the mid-1980s a high and rising U.S. external debt has aroused great concern, for two

Figure 2-2. Public Sector Debt-GNP Ratios in the Group of Seven Countries, 1975–1994

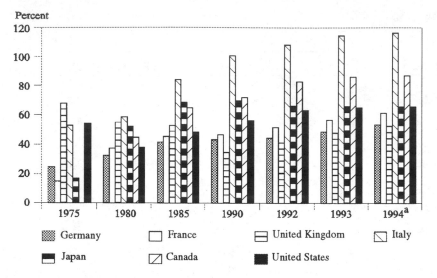

Source: OECD and Bundesministerium für Finanzen.
a. Estimated.

Figure 2-3. Public Sector Debt-GNP Ratio in the Smaller EU Countries, 1976–1993

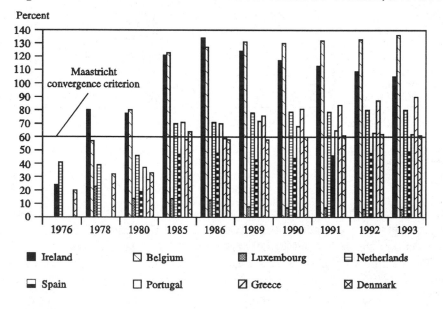

Source: Country submissions.

primary reasons. First, in the 1980s both the federal deficit and the federal debt grew dramatically. The latter increased from about 34 percent of GNP in 1980 to over 55 percent in 1989 and is expected to top 70 percent in 1995.[37] Given the low U.S. saving rate, which constrains the United States' ability to finance government deficits internally, this has led to higher real interest rates, hence strong capital inflows, and thus, as their counterpart, a rising foreign trade deficit and a considerable increase in federal (net) external indebtedness. Between 1980 and 1992 the external debt of the United States rose from $118 billion to $549 billion, or from 4.4 percent to 9.1 percent of GDP. The federal government's share of the overall debt rose from 15 percent in 1982 to 20 percent in 1992. Against the background of high interest rates, initially intended to reduce inflation, and a strong dollar, this sharp increase was commonly seen as one of the reasons for the high unemployment and slow growth in the United States during the early 1990s.[38]

Second, there is rising concern in the United States that its growing external debt will force the country either to remit an increasing amount of its national income to foreigners or to experience a flood of foreign purchases of domestic assets.[39] If current trends in external borrowing continue, foreign net claims on the United States will amount to 20 percent of GNP, and about 2 percent of GNP will go to foreigners by the year 2000.[40]

For the time being, the situation in the Federal Republic appears much more favorable. It is true that the external public sector debt has increased from about DM 220 billion in 1990 to DM 348 billion in 1992, or from 20.9 percent to 25.9 percent of the total debt. But the net international creditor position of the Federal Republic has actually improved, from DM 325.4 billion to DM 338.1 billion, during the same time period.[41] A considerable number of these creditors are German citizens who have invested their funds abroad, encouraged most recently by revisions in German taxation of interest income.[42]

The term structure of the German public debt has also changed, with long-term obligations assuming an increased share of the total (table 2-8).[43] Whereas treasury bills and bonds and government bonds made up 27 percent of the overall debt in 1985, their share had increased to 40 percent by 1992. This rising share of longer term debt instruments was most pronounced at the federal level, where the increase was from about DM 190 billion, or 48 percent, to DM 498 billion, or 78 percent of the total. Bond issues, most of which took place in international capital markets, provided the largest share, with an increase of almost DM 200 billion.[44]   At the state level the term structure changed only slightly, as the share of long-term debt instruments increased

Table 2-8. Structure of Public Debt, 1989–1993

	Indebtedness[a] (billions of DM)					Change from previous year (percentages)				
	1989	1990	1991	1992	1993[b]	1989	1990	1991	1992	1993[b]
Note Loans	496.0	517.0	549.3	546.4	604.0	-6.7	21.0	32.2	7.9	39.5
Securities	414.9	518.6	602.4	697.4	817.5	32.9	103.6	83.9	95.0	120.0
Other debts	17.9	17.0	22.1	83.5	88.0	-0.3	0.0	4.2	68.5	4.5
Total	928.8	1,053.5	1,173.9	1,345.2	1,509.5	25.8	124.7	102.4	171.4	164.0
Federal Government	490.5	542.2	586.5	611.1	685.5	15.4	51.6	44.3	24.6	74.0
Länder, west	309.9	328.8	347.4	366.6	394.0	7.3	18.9	18.6	19.2	27.5
Länder, east	...	...	4.9	22.5	40.0	...	...	4.9	17.6	17.5
Communities, west	112.9	116.5	132.1	141.3	152.5	1.6	3.6	6.5	9.3	11.0
Communities, east	...	...	8.6	13.2	20.0	...	...	8.6	4.6	7.0
German Unity Fund	...	19.8	50.5	74.4	87.5	...	19.8	30.7	23.9	13.5
Credit Liquidation Fund	...	27.6	27.5	91.7	101.0	...	27.6	-0.2	64.3	9.5
ERP Fund	7.1	9.5	16.4	24.3	28.5	1.1	2.4	6.9	7.9	4.0
Memoranda										
Treuhandanstalt	...	4.4	39.4	106.8	168.5	...	4.4	25.3	67.4	61.5
Railways	44.1	48.4	43.1	53.5	66.0	1.4	4.3	-5.3	10.4	12.5
Post Office	66.2	71.0	81.3	96.6	104.5	2.0	4.8	10.3	15.4	8.0

Source: Deutsche Bundesbank.
a. At year's end.
b. Partially estimated.

from about 4 percent to 7 percent. The already minimal share of such instruments in the debt of western German communities dropped further, from 1.6 percent to 1 percent. This change stemmed from a number of factors, ranging from changes in the term structure of interest rates to institutional regulations.[45] A detailed forecast of the future term structure of the debt is beyond the scope of this analysis. But even if the current term structure is generally maintained, the share of long-term debt instruments will increase further until 1997, not least because the federal government will take on some of the debt issued by the Treuhandanstalt, the German Unity Fund, and other agencies. It is therefore unlikely that the term structure of the public sector budgets contains any risk potential in the foreseeable future.[46]

MACROECONOMIC EFFECTS. The goal of Germany's federal, state, and local governments—to reduce the federal deficit from 5 percent to 1.8 percent of GNP between 1993 and 1997—is very ambitious, especially compared with consolidation efforts in the United States. Between 1975 and 1980 the Federal Republic went through a similar retrenchment, when the deficit-GNP ratio was cut from 5.6 percent to 2.6 percent. Between 1981 and 1989 the consolidation of federal finances was even more pronounced: a deficit of 3.8 percent of GNP was transformed into a surplus of 0.1 percent. In both instances, however, the period over which the reductions were achieved was longer than that now being contemplated, and the international setting probably more favorable.

If the contractionary effects on the economy are used as the basis for comparison, the pending policy measures are less intrusive than the most ambitious consolidation program of the Federal Republic to date—the so-called Operation '82. The contractionary effects of this program were about DM 19 billion (1.2 percent of GNP) in 1982 and DM 23 billion (1.4 percent of GNP) in 1983.[47] This compares with a contraction of 0.5 percent of GNP in 1994, caused by an increase in the fuel tax, social security contributions, and the introduction of long-term care and nursing insurance; and with about 2 percent (assumed) in 1995, caused by the 7.5 percent solidarity surcharge (*Solidaritätsbeitrag*) on personal and corporate income taxes (expected to raise DM 28 billion in revenues), an increase in the wealth tax from 0.5 percent to 1 percent (DM 1 billion), and a further increase of the insurance tax from 12 percent to 15 percent (DM 2.4 billion). The following sections discuss the implications for the expenditure and revenue sides of the budget.

EXPENDITURES. As of this writing, the medium-term financial plan of the federal government projects an average increase in federal expenditures of 2.3 percent annually between 1993 and 1997.[48] This rate is 2.7 percentage points below the federal government's forecast for nominal GNP/GDP growth. In recent history the federal government has been able to keep expenditure increases at rates below the growth of GNP for several years in succession only between 1983 and 1986, when on average GNP grew by 5 percent and government expenditures by 3.5 percent.

Cuts in the 1994 federal budget focus primarily on the following areas. First, a limit has been placed on federal expenditures, to be realized primarily through a salary freeze for civil servants. Second, the budget calls for a continued reduction of subsidies in western Germany in all important areas (agriculture, manufacturing, and mining), with the exception of housing. The intention is to cut subsidies by 10 percent, which should lead to a balancing of financial aid given to the old and the new Länder. A third area targeted for budget cuts is labor market policies and the Federal Employment Agency. According to the federal government, measures in this area are intended to achieve an appropriate reduction of unemployment benefits and the deadweight effects as well as a redistribution of the fiscal burden of liabilities, keeping existing interests in mind.[49] Finally, the federal government intends to cut spending on family policies, social services, and education by linking benefits more closely to the recipients' incomes. Additional savings—DM 2 billion in 1994 and DM 5 billion in 1995—are anticipated from deterring tax evasion and from legislation to repeal unfair tax privileges. The federal government hopes to "compensate the unavoidable additional expenditures in the consumption area for the most part with cuts in consumption. This will allow a continued high level of investment expenditures in order to strengthen the economic recovery in Germany, especially in the new Länder."[50]

The government's projections for individual budget categories until 1997 are shown in table 2-9. (Similar data for state and local budgets are not currently available.) The projections show that the following areas will be particularly affected by cuts: labor market policy (DM 8 billion), defense (DM 8.8 billion), promotion of economic development (gross cuts of DM 4 billion), nutrition, agriculture, and forestry (DM 3.8 billion), transportation and communications (DM 2.1 billion), science and research and development, excluding the universities (DM 1 billion), and the "other expenditures" category (DM 6 billion), which includes economic cooperation and federal aid for Berlin. Expenditure increases are primarily planned for the pension insurance of blue and white collar workers, small and medium-sized enterprise promotion, regional economic aid, credit guarantees, debt service and credit procurement costs (DM 25 billion), amortization of old debts in the eastern German housing

Table 2-9. Expenditures of the Federal Government by Function, 1992-1997

Millions of DM except where stated otherwise

	1992	1993	1994	1995	1996	1997	*Average annual rate of change 1992–97* %
Social Security	146,679	168,200	168,281	166,593	161,003	157,548	1.4
Pension insurance of wage earners, salaried employees, miners	59,973	65,257	74,263	75,662	76,963	79,147	5.7
Labor market policy, job protection	25,385	40,458	32,983	29,132	23,051	17,296	-7.4
Education allowance, maternity protection, family policy	7,966	7,876	7,619	9,326	9,623	9,621	3.8
Child benefits	21,987	21,850	20,390	20,390	20,390	20,390	-1.5
Housing allowance	3,704	3,656	3,552	2,859	2,759	2,700	-6.1
Residential construction subsidies	577	550	450	350	320	320	-11.1
Benefits and pensions payable to war victims	13,038	13,701	14,134	14,125	13,429	13,195	0.2
Reparations, refunds, equalization of burdens	2,144	2,001	1,790	1,732	1,651	1,595	-5.7
Social security for farmers	6,419	6,830	7,217	7,556	8,005	8,444	5.6
Other social policy measures	5,486	6,021	5,883	5,461	4,812	4,840	-2.5
Defense	57,009	53,727	51,407	49,318	48,794	48,602	-3.1
Defense	53,327	50,413	48,977	47,570	47,570	47,570	-2.3
Defense costs due to the presence of foreign forces	2,814	2,541	1,762	1,109	615	434	-31.2
Civil defense	868	773	668	639	609	598	-7.2
Food, agriculture, and forestry	8,082	6,775	5,977	5,126	4,529	4,343	-11.7
Joint task "Improvement of agrarian structure and coastal protection"	3,011	3,210	2,965	2,720	2,640	2,450	-4.0
Other measures in agriculture	5,071	3,565	3,012	2,406	1,889	1,893	-17.9
Promotion of economic development	17,734	22,742	20,517	25,088	23,390	23,331	5.6
Energy sector	4,410	4,237	3,181	2,255	1,945	2,234	-12.7
Other sectoral promotion	2,505	1,859	1,666	1,376	1,298	1,200	-13.7
Small and medium-sized enterprises	1,166	1,542	1,925	2,575	2,842	2,984	20.7
Regional economic development	4,937	6,149	5,182	11,926	10,491	10,220	15.7
Industrial research	322	426	514	402	330	266	-3.7
Guarantees and other measures to promote economic development	4,394	8,529	8,049	6,554	6,484	6,427	7.9

Table 2-9. (cont.) Expenditures of the Federal Government by Function, 1992-1997

Millions of DM except where stated otherwise

	1992	1993	1994	1995	1996	1997	Average annual rate of change 1992–97 %
Transportation and communication	40,061	45,409	54,679	55,953	60,276	60,040	8.1
Federal railways and railway reform	20,607	22,812	32,348	33,680	40,913	40,669	14.6
Railways - federal office	...	...	122	122	121	121	...
Federal highways	9,859	10,757	10,757	10,600	10,600	10,600	1.5
Improvement of transport conditions in communities, local transport	4,769	6,280	6,280	6,280	3,280	3,280	-7.2
Waterways, ports	2,473	2,808	2,891	3,049	3,142	3,122	4.8
Postal service, news media, and telecommunications	1,120	1,434	1,153	1,127	1,130	1,131	0.2
Research, educational, and cultural affairs	20,193	20,997	19,615	19,265	19,130	18,969	-1.2
Science R&D (excluding higher education)	12,019	11,981	11,859	11,882	12,013	12,041	0.0
Joint task "Enlargement and construction of institutions of higher learning (incl. university hospitals)," special programs for higher education	1,929	2,291	2,265	2,158	2,006	1,897	-0.3
Job training, promotion of junior scientists	2,968	3,103	2,836	2,709	2,640	2,579	-2.8
Occupational education, other areas of education, cultural affairs	3,277	3,622	2,655	2,516	2,471	2,452	-5.6

ing sector, the Credit Liquidation Fund, and the debt settlement fund (an additional DM 23.4 billion). Debt service would amount to DM 68.6 billion by 1997, or about 16.6 percent of total expenditures, compared with 9.7 percent in 1989 and 12.2 percent in 1992. This means that debt service would not only exceed planned investments (DM 65.7 billion) by DM 3 billion[51] but also surpass net borrowing (DM 38 billion) by 70 percent. The share of public sector wages, salaries, and pensions in total expenditures would decrease from 11.4 percent to 10.4 percent. Assuming that growth in public sector earnings remains below that in the overall economy, the number of government employ-

Table 2-9. (cont.) Expenditures of the Federal Government by Function, 1992-1997

Millions of DM except where stated otherwise

	1992	1993	1994	1995	1996	1997	Average annual rate of change 1992–97 %
Other expenditures	136,867	140,293	157,925	157,657	171,880	187,171	6.5
Housing, urban construction, regional development	3,266	3,247	4,096	5,040	5,582	5,625	11.5
Environmental protection, health care, sports and recreation	1,944	2,150	2,217	2,200	2,145	2,105	1.6
Safety, public order, asylum	3,502	4,187	4,271	4,340	4,382	4,231	3.9
Economic cooperation	8,172	8,344	8,226	8,217	8,355	8,525	0.8
Federal aid to Berlin, relocation of parliament and government	13,728	10,743	6,484	591	595	687	-45.1
Interest, credit procurement costs	44,080	45,692	53,381	57,124	62,124	69,118	9.4
Maintenance	13,121	13,457	14,341	14,471	14,546	14,636	2.2
German Unity Fund	15,019	27,724	38,619	9,524	9,526	9,529	-8.7
Treuhandanstalt	...	...	...	7,500	7,500	7,500	...
Redemption and servicing of housing debt, Credit Liquidation Fund, Debt Redemption Fund	7,648	6,450	8,350	29,775	29,600	30,000	31.4
Others	26,837	19,467	18,040	17,262	18,930	20,385	-5.0
Unspecified expenditures and savings	...	-1,168	-100	1,613	8,595	14,830	...
Total	427,165	458,143	478,401	479,000	489,002	500,004	3.2

Source: Bundesministerium der Finanzen, *Finanzbericht 1994*, pp. 58ff, and authors' calcualtions. Figures for 1992 and 1993 are from actual budgets, those for 1994 and 1995 from the draft budgets, and those for 1996 and 1997 are from the ministry's financial planning.

ees would have to decline by about 2 percent. Expenditures for general government and administration, on the other hand, would increase by almost 25 percent, from DM 10.4 billion to DM 12.9 billion.

In evaluating the government's plan it is necessary to realize that most, if not all, of the additional expenditures are targeted for the new Länder. The old Länder therefore are likely to face real and possibly even nominal cuts. The cuts in public sector investments will affect, most of all, local public transportation (a reduction of DM 2.3 billion), defense (DM 0.7 billion), subsidies to home construction (DM 0.3 billion), investments related to the government's move to Berlin (DM 0.3 billion), and the "other" category (more than DM 9 billion); the sharp decline in this last category is due to the cessation of the Partnership for Eastern Renewal (Gemeinschaftswerk Aufschwung Ost). Potential uncertainties in the federal government's projected expenditures arise from the need to support the reform process in Eastern Europe and to manage political refugees and the integration of ethnic Germans.[52]   Whether the Federal Republic's net contribution to deepening European integration will be considerably higher than expected is also currently an open question.[53]

The relationship between investment and consumption expenditures is often seen as central to fiscal and macroeconomic policy considerations. In the government's plan the share of investment in overall expenditures will decrease from 14.8 percent in 1993 to 13.1 percent by 1997 (table 2-10).[54] Total investment expenditures will be flat in nominal terms over the 1992 97 period, and some categories in which higher expenditures might be expected to spur economic growth, such as local transport and student loan programs, will even decline. As already noted, however, the bulk of the reductions (more than DM 9 billion) is concentrated in the "other" category, where individual cuts are hard for third parties to identify. According to the government, the reason for this distribution of cuts, which is unsatisfactory from a growth perspective, is the dynamic behavior of consumption expenditures. Their net increase despite projected cuts in personnel compensation is due primarily to mounting debt service, appropriations, and subsidies (contrary to what one might expect, subsidies are not categorized as investments). At the state and local level the situation appears to be very much the same, although detailed information is not readily available.[55]

REVENUES. Between 1994 and 1997 total tax revenues are expected to increase by an annual average of 7 percent. State revenue will increase at an above-average rate of about 7.6 percent per year, while the federal government and local communities will see revenue growth remain at below-average rates of 6.7 percent and 6.3 percent per year, respectively. Part of this increase is due to tax increases, elimination of tax privileges, and measures to prevent the abuse of the tax system. For example, the solidarity surcharge will collect additional tax revenues of DM 28 billion, compensating for about half of the cyclical tax shortfalls between 1993 and 1997. Without these tax hikes, the increase in revenues would only amount to 5.6 percent annually. As a result of the cyclical shortfalls and their partial compensation through new tax increases, the tax struc-

Table 2-10. Investment Expenditures of the Federal Government, Actual and Projected, 1992–1997

Millions of DM except where stated otherwise

	1992	1993	1994	1995	1996	1997	*Average annual rate of change 1992–97* %
Federal railways	8,076	9,599	10,110	10,835	10,921	10,786	6.0
Federal highways	7,977	8,822	8,766	8,527	8,531	8,529	1.3
Guarantees	4,071	8,000	7,500	6,000	6,000	6,000	8.1
Development aid	6,490	6,678	6,635	6,625	6,758	6,927	1.3
Municipal road construction	1,847	5,015	5,015	5,015	2,617	2,617	7.2
Joint task "Regional economic structure"	2,984	4,056	4,306	4,606	3,206	2,950	-0.2
Research	2,552	2,908	2,889	2,922	2,919	2,914	2.7
Residential construction in Germany	1,630	2,129	2,447	2,726	2,972	3,062	13.4
Residential construction in former USSR	1,253	2,225	1,972	350	...	...	...
Joint task "Agrarian structure and coastal protection"	1,862	1,865	1,710	1,630	1,630	1,630	-2.6
Joint task "Enlargement and construction of institutions of higher learning"	1,600	1,680	1,680	1,600	1,600	1,600	0.0
Local transport	2,913	1,254	1,254	1,254	654	654	-25.8
Federal waterways	826	1,051	1,056	1,203	1,315	1,308	9.6
Student loan program (BAföG)	993	960	860	815	815	815	-3.9
Defense (incl. civil defense and stationing/withdrawal of foreign forces)	961	909	802	763	707	690	-6.4
Environmental protection, nature conservation	594	693	772	783	746	680	2.7
Urban construction	748	635	750	872	829	763	0.4
Federal properties	626	575	676	718	709	706	2.4
Residential construction premium	577	550	450	350	320	320	-11.1
Investments in conjunction with the relocation of parliament and government	867	818	448	619	454	494	-10.6
Investment and financial aid to Länder	1,500	1,500	...	6,600	6,600	6,600	34.5
Other expenditures	14,870	5,937	4,732	4,392	5,293	5,665	-17.6
Total	65,816	67,856	64,828	69,208	65,596	65,712	-0.0
Increase from previous year (percentages)		3.1	-4.5	6.8	-5.2	0.2	...
Share of total expenditures (percentages)		14.8	13.6	14.4	13.4	13.1	...

Source: Bundesministerium der Finanzen, *Finanzbericht 1994*, pp. 58ff, and authors' calcualtions. Figures for 1992 and 1993 are from actual budgets, those for 1994 and 1995 from draft budgets, and those for 1996 and 1997 are from the ministry's financial planning.

Figure 2-4. Direct and Indirect Taxes in Germany, 1980–1997[a]

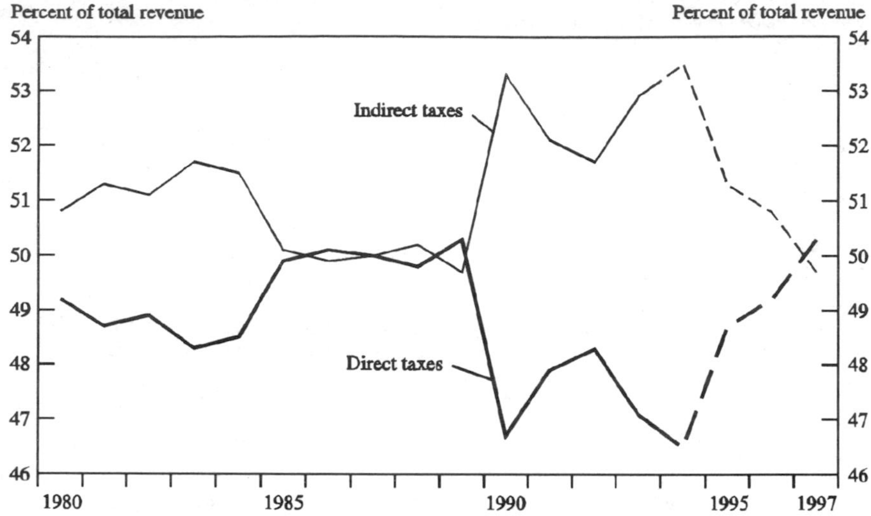

Percent of total revenue   Percent of total revenue

Source: Authors' calculations.
a. Figures for 1980-1990 are for West-Germany only. Dashed lines indicate estimates.

ture will also change. Whereas the composition of direct and indirect taxes (the latter consist mainly of VAT and excise taxes) in the western German budget was 47-53 in the early 1990s, it will be almost balanced by 1997 (figure 2-4). The share of direct taxes will be considerably higher in eastern Germany, and only marginally higher in Germany as a whole.

Given these tax increases and the reorganization of federal revenue sharing, the shares of the different levels of government will also change, with the Länder emerging as the beneficiaries. Their share of total tax revenue will increase from 31.1 percent in 1992 to 36.3 percent in 1997, at the expense of the federal government, whose share will decline by 1.6 percent (table 2-11). The federal government will also take over some additional financial burdens from the western German Länder, resulting in an increase of the capital stock of the German Unity Fund in 1993-94 and in a new system of revenue sharing among the Länder that will come into effect after 1995. Local communities are also among the losers: their share of overall tax revenue will drop by 0.6 percent.

As on the expenditure side, there are some potentially risky "unknowns" on the revenue side. These include the still-pending reform of the rules governing

Table 2-11. Tax Revenues of Federal, State, and Local Governments, Actual and Projected, 1992–1997

Year and level of government	Millions of DM	Share of total tax revenues (percentages)	Change from previous year (percentages)
1992			
Federal government	386,814	52.9	...
State government	251,023	34.3	...
Local government	93,257	12.8	...
Total	731	100.0	...
1993			
Federal government	392,619	52.4	1.5
State government	260,397	34.5	3.7
Local government	95,943	12.8	2.9
Total	748,959	100.0	2.4
1994			
Federal government	411,215	52.5	4.7
State government	275,879	35.2	5.9
Local government	96,605	12.3	0.7
Total	783,699	100.0	4.6
1995			
Federal government	439,138	52.0	6.8
State government	304,550	36.0	10.4
Local government	101,412	12.0	5.0
Total	845,100	100.0	7.8
1996			
Federal government	464,009	51.7	5.7
State government	324,713	36.2	6.6
Local government	109,283	12.1	7.8
Total	898,095	100.0	6.3
1997			
Federal government	489,166	51.4	5.4
State government	344,554	36.2	6.1
Local government	118,481	12.4	8.4
Total	952,201	100.0	6.0

Source: Authors' calculations.

income tax exemptions (e.g., the proposal to raise the subsistence minimum income that is exempt from tax) and the *Vorsorgepauschale* (a lump-sum deductible for retirement planning), but also the new regulation governing the taxation of income from interest. Whereas these measures will reduce revenues, planned increases in real estate property taxes (through the adjustment of assessed values) will increase them.

IMPLICATIONS FOR PRIVATE HOUSEHOLDS. Obviously the private sector, and ultimately private households, will always be affected by any government decision to use more resources or to cut its deficit, whether it achieves these aims through higher taxes, through reducing the real supply or increasing the prices of public commodities and services, or through further indebtedness. Each of these policies has, of course, different consequences, for example with respect to the interpersonal or intergenerational distribution of the rising burden. (Intergenerational issues lie beyond the scope of this analysis, given its comparatively short time horizon.)

Leaving expenditure cuts aside and concentrating on the tax measures taken or envisioned, it becomes apparent that the transfers within the social security system played a major role, and up to 1993 *the* major role, in aggregate western German transfers to eastern Germany (tables 2-12 and 2-13). As a consequence, employees liable to social security contributions had to bear more than their share of the fiscal transfers. In 1992 blue collar workers contributed 4 percent and white collar 4.5 percent of their gross income, while for the self-employed and civil servants this share reached only 2 percent (figure 2-5). Retired persons contributed only slightly more than 2 percent, mainly because they are exempt from contributing to pension and unemployment insurance. The burden was slightly regressive: the lowest quartile of the income hierarchy paid about 3.2 percent of its gross income, and the highest 5 percent about 2.2 percent (table 2-14).[56]

In 1993 the west-to-east transfer within the unemployment insurance scheme was reduced from DM 24.6 billion to DM 15.1 billion by increasing the federal contribution from DM 13.8 billion to DM 25 billion. Because of the worsening employment situation in eastern Germany, its pension system incurred a DM 8.8 billion deficit, which had to be covered by its western German counterpart. As a consequence the west-to-east transfer within the social security system was reduced by only DM 5 billion.

On January 1, 1993, the (full) rate of the VAT was increased from 14 percent to 15 percent. Greater reliance on this regressive tax meant that high-income groups thus benefited further, as the solidarity surcharge had been lifted by mid-1992. By 1994, however, the direction of redistribution had changed. Although redistribution within the social security system still exceeds DM 30 billion, its share of total transfers will be diminished. With the reintroduction of the solidarity surcharge by January 1, 1995, the share of the social security system will be further reduced to about one-third of the additional taxes, which is still more than the shares of the increases in fuel taxes and the solidarity surcharge. Altogether, by 1995—and if

Table 2-12. Changes in Tax and Contribution Rates, 1991–1995[a]

Date of change	Tax or contribution	Change
1 April 1991	Unemployment insurance	Increase of contribution rate from 4.3 percent to 6.8 percent
	Pension insurance	Decrease of contribution rate from 18.7 percent to 17.7 percent
1 July 1991	Solidarity surcharge on income tax	Introduction of a 7.5 percent surcharge[b]
	Fuel tax	Increase of tax rate (e.g. for lead-free gasoline, from 60 to 82 pfennigs per liter)
	Insurance tax	Increase of tax rate from 7 percent to 10 percent
1 January 1992	Unemployment insurance	Decrease of contribution rate from 6.8 percent to 6.3 percent
1 March 1992	Tobacco tax	Increase of tax rate by about 1 pfennig per cigarette
3 June 1992	Solidarity surcharge	Cancellation of surcharge
1 January 1993	Value-added tax	Increase of full rate from 14 percent to 15 percent; reduced rate remains at 7 percent
	Pension insurance	Decrease of contribution rate from 17.7 percent to 17.5 percent
	Unemployment insurance	Increase of contribution rate from 6.3 percent to 6.5 percent
1 July 1993	Insurance tax	Increase of tax rate from 10 percent to 12 percent
1 January 1994	Pension insurance	Increase of contribution rate from 17.5 percent to 19.2 percent
	Fuel tax	Increase of tax rates (e.g. for lead-free gasoline, from 82 to 98 pfennigs per liter)
1 January 1995	Solidarity surcharge	Reintroduction of 7.5 percent surcharge
	Wealth tax	Increase of tax rate from 0.5 percent to 1.0 percent combined with a rise in the tax-exempt allowance
	Insurance tax	Increase of tax rate from 12 percent to 15 percent

Source: Authors' compilations
a. Only those charges that can be linked to the financing of German unification are listed; social security contributions include employer's share.
b. This amounts to an increase in the effective tax rate of 3.75 percent for 1991 and 1992.

Table 2-13. Financial Burdens on Western German Households from Public Transfers to Eastern Germany, 1991–1995

Billions of DM

Type of contribution (financial burden)	1991	1992	1993	1994	1995
Increases in taxes	16.7	24.8	26.1	38.5	69.0
Solidarity surcharge	11.0	10.2	0.2	0.6	27.7
Increases in					
Fuel tax[a]	5.2	12.7	14.1	22.9	22.8
Value-added tax	0.0	0.0	9.0	11.2	12.0
Insurance tax	0.5	1.3	1.9	2.6	4.2
Tobacco tax	0.0	0.6	0.9	1.2	1.2
Wealth tax	0.0	0.0	0.0	0.0	1.0
West-east transfers of social insurance	23.4	31.3	25.9	33.2	34.2
Unemployment insurance	21.6	24.6	15.1	17.4	18.0
Pension insurance	0.0	4.5	8.8	13.9	14.2
Payments for east German civil servants and pensioners[b]	1.8	2.2	2.0	1.9	2.0
All financial burdens	40.1	56.1	52.0	71.7	103.2
Memoranda: percentage shares of total financial burden					
Taxes	42.0	44.0	50.0	54.0	67.0
West-east transfers of social insurance	58.0	56.0	50.0	46.0	33.0

Source: Authors' calculations based on data from the federal ministries of Finance and of Labor and Social Affairs, as well as the Federal Statistical Office.

a. Includes the share of value-added tax contained in the increase; does not include the tax reduction resulting from the increase in the tax-deductible kilometer allowance.
b. Postponement of pay raises.

one ignores wage increases this will still be the case in 1997—the fiscal burden of financing unification will be more equally distributed among the various social and income groups than in 1992 (figure 2-5).

Federal revenues as a share of GNP will increase from about 45 percent in 1989 to about 50 percent in 1997 (table 2-5). The share of social security contributions will rise from 17.2 percent to 20 percent, and that of taxes from 25 percent to 30

Figure 2-5. Financial Burden on Selected Households, 1992 and 1995

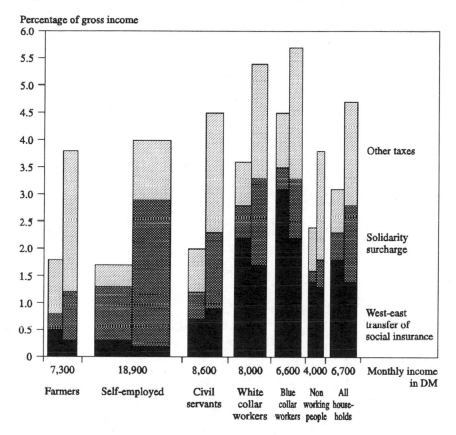

Percentage of gross income

Figure 2-5. Financial Burden on Selected Households, 1992 and 1995

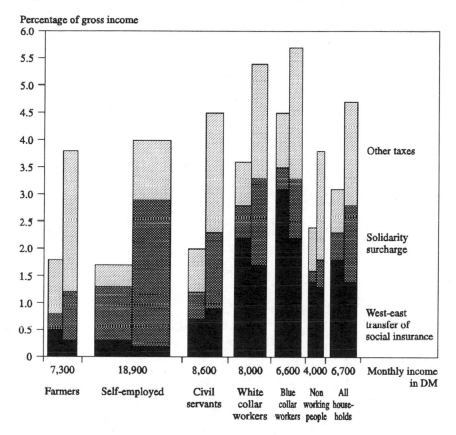

percent, hidden tax increases (bracket creep) will amount to about DM 80 billion, or about 3 percent, of the overall increase in tax revenues.

The increases in government-administered prices since 1989 have been directed primarily at the fuel tax (up 40 percent between 1989 to 1993) and the VAT (up 1 percentage point). As mentioned previously, these increases (and the rise in housing rents) are responsible for about one-third of the anticipated annual inflation rate of 3.5 percent between 1990 and 1993. The federal government expects a further annual increase in the consumer price index by 3 percent between 1993 and 1997. Given that the increase in public sector wages is expected to remain below the average increase for all workers, and assuming no increases in prices of imports, this means further price increases in the government sector.

Table 2-14. Financial Burden by Income Group from Tax Increases and the West-East Transfer of Social Insurance, 1992 and 1995

DM per month except where stated otherwise

Households grouped by income	Average income[a]	1992			1995			
		Total financial burden	Of which: West-east transfer of social insurance	Total burden as a share of income (percentages)	Total financial burden	Of which: West-east transfer of social insurance	Total burden as a share of income (percentages)	Total burden as a percentage of 1992 burden[b]
1st quartile	2,300	70	50	3.2	110	40	4.5	150
2nd quartile	4,300	160	100	3.7	230	90	5.1	150
3rd quartile	6,800	240	150	3.5	350	120	4.9	150
4th quartile	13,400	360	180	2.7	650	140	4.6	180
75–95 percentile	10,600	320	180	3.0	520	140	4.6	160
95–100 percentile	24,500	550	160	2.2	1,200	120	4.6	220
All households	6,700	210	120	3.1	340	100	4.7	160

Source: Authors' calculations based on data from the ministries of Finance and of Labor and Social Affairs, as well as the Federal Statistical Office.

a. For gross income in 1995 an across-the-board increase of 6.5 percent from 1992 levels is assumed.
b. Figures are rounded to the nearest 10 percent.

The contributions of expenditure cuts to financing unification, or to reducing the budget deficit, are difficult to assess accurately, especially as far as the share of or the impact on households and business is concerned. First, according to official policy statements, a policy of relative expenditure reduction, which was already being pursued in the years prior to unification, will be continued throughout the 1990s. For comparison, the 1989 budget projected growth in expenditures of about 3.1 percent per year for 1990 to 1993, assuming GNP growth of 4.5 percent and a 2 percent change in the GNP deflator.[57] Second, it is widely known that any implicit "savings" are not equally distributed across budget categories. In addition, it remains to be seen to what extent the cuts in funding will be offset by productivity improvements in the public sector. Such improvements may absorb some of the potential decline in public services. Again, it is not possible to link financial burdens for individual cases to households or the corporate sector. Finally, the distribution of expenditure cuts and increases between the new and the old Länder also remains unknown.[58]

As discussed previously, current plans for expenditure cuts (table 2-9) focus principally on the defense budget (about DM 10 billion in reductions from 1992 to 1997), the whole area of social security (labor market policy, labor protection, home construction subsidies, restitution, reimbursement, burden sharing, and others), and the area of research, education, science, and cultural affairs (educational grants, promotion of young scientists, apprenticeships, and other areas of cultural affairs and higher education). Private households are likely to bear about DM 25 billion of the almost DM 60 billion in (nominal) cuts in expenditures by 1997. In real terms, expenditures will drop by an average of 15 percent.

The impact of tax and price increases on different social and income groups is difficult to estimate for lack of sufficient information.[59] The introduction of a new tax code in 1996 will have important distributional consequences but cannot be examined yet because no policy decisions have been made. If the current marginal tax rates for each tax bracket remain the same, a revenue loss of DM 50 billion would be concomitant with the introduction of a higher level of exemption. This and a possible hike in taxes, or even a return of the hidden tax, would cause, among other things, a considerable shift of the tax burden from the upper to the middle and (if indirect taxes are raised to compensate for the revenue loss) lower income levels. In reorganizing the tax structure, the government could of course compensate any loss of tax revenues that resulted from higher exemption levels in the upper income tax brackets by raising the

Table 2-15. Distributional Effects of Alternative Tax Increases in Western Germany, 1991

DM per month

Households grouped by income	Average gross income	Average financial burden from:			Additional financial burden from:	
		Income tax	Value-added tax	Both	Surcharge on income tax[a]	Increase in value-added tax[b]
1st quartile	2,200	30	230	260	0	30
2nd quartile	4,100	370	420	790	30	60
3rd quartile	6,600	870	620	1,490	70	90
4th quartile	13,100	2,240	900	3,140	180	130
75–95 percentile	10,300	1,640	870	2,510	130	120
95–100 percentile	23,900	4,650	1,050	5,700	370	150
All households	6,500	880	540	1,420	70	80

Source: Authors' calculations based on data from the Federal Statistical Office.

a. Based on an 8 percent surcharge.
b. Based on a 2-percentage-point increase in the tax rate (to 14 percent)

marginal tax rates in the middle and upper income categories.

Past and future policy measures to increase government revenue, such as the proposed 7.5 percent surcharge on income taxes or keeping in place the hidden income taxes that have accumulated since the last tax reduction in 1990, are expected to relieve lower income households in relative terms (tables 2-15 and 2-16). An increase in social security insurance would have the opposite effect. The increase in insurance taxes and the already-implemented increase in fuel and tobacco taxes will also have regressive effects. The allocational effects will especially impact the east-west dimension of the redistribution. For the moment, eastern Germans generally pay a smaller than average share of income taxes and a higher than average share of consumption taxes. This pattern is the result not only of the lower incomes but also of the consumption patterns of eastern Germans, who still spend more on alcoholic beverages, tobacco, and gasoline than their western counterparts. On the other hand, eastern German households are less likely to be affected by the fuel tax, because the share of households that heat with oil in western Germany is considerably higher. The same is true for insurance taxes.

It is self-evident that the distributional effects of cuts in *monetary* transfers in the area of social security—the area that is most important here—are regressive. It is more difficult, however, to comment on the effects of expenditure policy decisions on *real transfers*.[60] In 1978 (more recent analyses are not available) the most important areas for real transfers were education, health, and transportation. Almost 70 percent of public expenditures, or 14 percent of GNP, were in these areas; 44 percent of these expenditures went for health services, 30 percent for education, and 26 percent for transportation. The same proportions probably prevail in western Germany today. It is likely that the incidence of benefits from expenditures in the areas of transportation and health is still regressive. In education, the rate of incidence at first is likely to be progressive, but for higher incomes it is regressive here as well.

The planned consolidation policies, with their relatively small modifications as measured by contribution levels, have hardly changed anything either. These policies are likely to have a regressive tendency. Marginal considerations therefore show that the burdens for the lower stratum of wage earners and transfer recipients are significant.

IMPLICATIONS FOR BUSINESSES. It is difficult to estimate the direct effects of federal expenditure cuts at the enterprise level, apart from minor items such as premiums on industry close research. Nevertheless, these policies will have an indirect effect on macroeconomic performance, as discussed above. For exam-

Table 2-16. Effects of Alternative Tax Increases on Selected Households, 1991
DM per month

	Single, no children		Single parent with one child		Married, one spouse working — one child		Married, one spouse working — four children		Married, both working — no children	
	East	West	East	West	East	West	East	West	East	West
Average gross pay	1,700	3,800	1,200	2,700	1,700	3,800	1,700	3,800	2,900	6,500
Less taxes withheld	120	640	0	130	0	320	0	180	160	970
Less social security contributions	300	670	210	480	300	670	300	670	520	1,150
Plus transfers[a]	10	0	110	70	70	70	800	660	30	0
Net income	1,290	2,490	1,100	2,160	1,470	2,880	2,200	3,610	2,250	4,380
Financial burdens due to increase in:										
Income tax[b]	10	50	0	10	0	30	0	10	10	80
Value-added tax[c]	20	30	20	30	20	40	40	50	40	60
Difference	-10	20	-20	-20	-20	-10	-40	-40	-30	20
Memoranda: ratio of east to west German incomes (percentages)										
Gross pay	45		44		45		45		45	
Net income	52		51		51		61		51	

Source: Authors' calculations based on the RWI distribution model.

a. Child benefits, employee savings allowance, residential construction subsidies.
b. Based on 8 percent surcharge on taxes withheld.
c. Based on 2-percentage-point increase in tax rate (to 14 percent)

ple, cutbacks in federal construction investment or federal consumption by DM 1 million over three years will reduce GNP by an average of DM 1.3 million to DM 1.7 million, according to calculations using the RWI econometric business cycle model; an increase in income taxes of the same magnitude will reduce GNP by DM 1.2 billion.[61]

INTERNATIONAL IMPLICATIONS. Some of the potential implications of German unification for the international economy have already been discussed. An overview of the importance of the Federal Republic for the pattern of growth in selected countries is shown in table 2-17. Detailed estimates of the effects of the consolidation strategies outlined here are not yet available and lie beyond the scope of this analysis.

An analysis by Warwick McKibbin of the Brookings Institution arrives at growth effects from the consolidation strategies of about 1.3 percentage points, inflation effects of about 1 percentage point, and an increase in long-term real interest rates of about 1 percentage point for the rest of the EMS countries.[62] In an updated version, with assumptions concerning deficit reduction similar to those developed here, McKibbin calculates a decisive growth effect for the other EMS countries. But he also assumes the continuing absorption of the eastern German work force by the unified Germany through a reduction of real wages as well as a devaluation of the deutsche mark within the EMS area (in 2018 by 20 percent), accompanied by a lowering of interest rates in these same countries.[63] In the other OECD countries, growth effects are less than -0.2 percentage point and long-term real interest rates increase by 1 percentage point. The developing countries, Eastern Europe, and the OPEC countries are affected only through the terms of trade.

More general implications can be derived from a comprehensive and detailed analysis of the international consequences of national fiscal and monetary policy measures in the OECD area. In the second half of the 1980s, a study conducted under the auspices of the Brookings Institution examined the most important fiscal and monetary policy implications of 12 prominent international models. We will not elaborate here on the details of these models—their theoretical foundation, their empirical basis, their international transmission mechanisms, or problems with the implementation of the policy measures they assume.[64] The results presented below are based on average results calculated by the editors of the Brookings study and are limited to the fiscal and monetary policy impulses of the OECD countries excluding the United States ("rest of OECD," or ROECD), and the effects on real GNP and the inflation rate (according to the price index for private consumption) in the United States, the ROECD, the Federal Republic, France,

Table 2-17. Germany's Importance for Economic Growth in Selected Countries

| Country | Exports to Germany[a] | | Multipliers | | |
	As a percentage of total German imports	Billions of 1980 DM	Exports (DM billion)[b]	Imports (DM billion)[c]	Government expenditures (percentages)[d]
United States	6.8	0.7	1.74	0.26	1.59
Japan	5.8	0.6	1.02	0.45	...
France	11.5	1.3	0.77	0.60	2.82
United Kingdom	7.2	0.8	1.00	0.35	1.54
Italy	8.9	1.0	2.10	0.60	...
Netherlands	11.1	1.2	0.71	...	...
Belgium	6.9	0.8	0.71	...	...
Canada	0.8	0.1	1.47	...	...
Austria	4.0	0.4	1.00	...	...
Finland	1.0	0.1	1.4	...	...
Sweden	2.4	0.3	0.78	...	...

Source: Federal Statistical Office; B. G. Hickman and V. Filatov, "A Decomposition of International Income Multipliers," in F. G. Adams and B. G. Hickman (eds.), *Global Econometrics: Essays in Honor of Lawrence R. Klein* (Cambridge, MA: 1983), p.362, table 2-7; and P. Bekx, and others, "The QUEST Model (Version 1988)," *Economic Papers*, 75 (Brussels: EC Commission, 1989), p.60.

a. Figures are averages for 1985–1989. The absolute amounts calculated are based on the regional structure using average growth rates of Germany's imports.
b. Increase in real GDP in response to a DM 1 billion increase in real exports from Germany (see Hickman and Filatov), as estimated for 1979.
c. Increase in real GDP in response to to a DM 1 billion increase in real imports to Germany (see Hickman and Filatov), as estimated for 1979.
d. Increase in real GDP in response to a 1 percent increase in public sector investment in Germany, assuming fixed money supply and constant exchange rates (see Bekx and others).

the United Kingdom, and Italy. For purposes of comparison the effects of a devaluation of the U.S. dollar are also shown (table 2-18).

The fiscal stimulus involves a consistent increase in federal expenditures by 1 percent of real GNP for every ROECD country for the years 1985 to 1990. For the Federal Republic this amounts to DM 18 billion per year and leads to an average

Table 2-18. Macroeconomic Implications for Selected OECD Countries of Changes in Economic Policies in Selected Global Models

Percentage change from base[a]

	Year 1	Year 2	Year 3	Year 4	Year 5	Year 6	Average
			Change in Fiscal Policy (ROECD)				
GNP (real)							
United States	0.22	0.19	0.10	0.06	-0.01	-0.07	0.10
ROECD	1.25	1.45	1.47	1.42	1.36	1.27	1.40
Germany	1.50	1.50	1.60	1.60	1.50	1.20	1.50
France	1.70	1.60	1.40	1.30	1.20	1.10	1.40
United Kingdom	1.10	1.10	1.10	1.10	1.20	1.20	1.10
Italy	1.20	1.50	1.50	1.50	1.40	1.30	1.40
Inflation							
United States	0.19	0.48	0.76	1.01	1.23	1.47	0.90
ROECD	0.03	0.35	0.74	1.11	1.53	2.01	0.90
Germany	0.40	-0.10	0.30	0.20	0.50	0.80	0.20
France	0.20	0.10	0.40	0.80	1.30	1.80	0.70
United Kingdom	0.00	0.40	0.90	1.50	2.10	2.80	1.30
Italy	0.10	0.30	0.70	1.10	1.60	2.00	1.00
			Change in Monetary Policy (ROECD)				
GNP (real)							
United States	0.14	0.31	0.22	0.32	0.27	0.27	0.20
ROECD	0.68	0.70	0.83	0.76	0.68	0.63	0.70
Germany	0.70	1.10	1.10	0.90	0.60	0.60	0.80
France	0.60	1.10	1.00	0.60	0.50	0.60	0.70
United Kingdom	0.10	0.30	0.20	0.20	0.20	0.20	0.20
Italy	0.20	0.40	0.50	0.50	0.50	0.50	0.40
Inflation							
United States	-0.33	-0.60	-0.70	-0.71	-0.68	-0.63	-0.60
ROECD	0.27	0.60	0.89	1.16	1.38	1.49	0.50
Germany	0.60	1.50	1.80	2.10	2.30	2.50	1.80
France	0.20	0.60	1.00	1.20	1.30	1.20	0.90
United Kingdom	0.50	0.90	1.30	1.50	1.70	1.80	1.30
Italy	0.50	1.00	1.20	1.40	1.60	1.90	1.30

Table 2-18. (cont.) Macroeconomic Implications for Selected OECD Countries of Changes in Economic Policies in Selected Global Models

Percentage change from base[a]

	Year 1	Year 2	Year 3	Year 4	Year 5	Year 6	Average
		Exogenous Depreciation of U.S. Dollar					
GNP (real)							
United States	0.16	0.42	0.72	0.69	0.72	0.55	0.50
ROECD	-0.28	-0.71	-1.23	-1.60	-1.85	-1.96	...
Germany	-0.20	-0.70	-1.80	-2.80	-3.80	-3.90	-2.20
France	-0.00	0.40	1.20	2.30	3.40	4.50	-0.30
United Kingdom	-0.20	-0.50	-1.00	-1.30	-1.20	-1.10	-0.90
Italy	-0.20	-0.60	-1.20	-1.40	-1.10	-1.00	-0.90
Inflation							
United States	0.27	0.95	1.99	3.32	4.13	5.09	2.00
ROECD	-0.30	-1.09	-2.26	-3.42	-4.31	-5.09	0.80
Germany	-0.10	-0.30	-0.60	-1.10	-1.60	-2.10	-3.10
France	-0.20	-1.00	-2.30	-3.80	-4.80	-5.80	-3.00
United Kingdom	-0.60	-2.10	-3.80	-5.30	-6.30	-7.10	-4.20
Italy	-0.40	-1.50	-3.20	-4.80	-5.80	-6.50	-3.70

Source: R. C. Bryant and others (eds.), *Empirical Macroeconomics for Interdependent Economies*, supplemental volume (Brookings, 1988), and authors' calculations.

a. For descriptions of the simulations see the text.
b. ROECD consists of the OECD countries except the United States.

annual GNP increase of 1.5 percent. The effects are smaller for the other OECD countries, and for the United States they can even be ignored. France and Italy experience effects similar to those in Germany, while those for the United Kingdom are smaller. The rate of inflation in the Federal Republic rises by about 0.2 percentage point on average. For the United States and the rest of the OECD countries, especially the European countries, the inflation effects are considerably higher. A comparison of the effects of a joint stimulus by particular countries and regions versus isolated national policy measures—for example, the above-mentioned multiplier results for the Federal Republic—reveals that the spillover effects are relatively small.

To estimate the effects of a monetary policy stimulus, an increase in the money supply by 2 percent in the first year and 4 percent in the second year in all of the ROECD countries was assumed. The result in the Federal Republic is an increase in real GNP that is notably higher than those in Italy and the United Kingdom and, of course, the United States. With respect to the inflation rate the results are reversed. Thus, despite its faster GNP growth, the inflationary effect of expansive monetary policy in the Federal Republic would be greater than in the ROECD countries.

Dollar devaluation (by 25 percent cumulatively between 1985 and 1987, maintained through 1990) affects Germany disproportionately, according to the model, especially when the comparison is with the other European countries; the differences are much smaller, however, with respect to the inflation rate.

Summary

The status quo forecast and anticipated developments in the federal budget indicate the following. First, although the Federal Republic will experience an absolute and relative decline in its public sector deficits from now until 1997, they will remain substantial. Tax rates and other contributions will remain at historically high levels, despite continuous reductions in federal services and transfer payments. Second, the gross national debt of the Federal Republic has reached an unprecedented level. Any latitude for policy action, for example to stimulate the economy, appears virtually nonexistent; the scope for action is very limited from a structural perspective as well, because the share of interest payments in total federal expenditures continues to increase. Third, the combination of a continued increase in tax rates and other contributions, with only slight improvements in real gross per capita income in the years to come, will cause stagnation or even a decline in real net income for large sections of the population, not to mention the implications of reduced federal services for their living conditions. Fourth, a considerable part of the planned expenditure cuts is likely to further reduce growth prospects, at least in western Germany.

III. What Could Be Done?

Within this dim overall economic perspective, the question of the impact a significant deficit reduction would have or to what extent it is responsible for such a situation, arises. The modest growth of German per capita income in recent years is primarily the result of slow growth in productivity relative to past western German experience.[1] The fact that part of the gains from such productivity growth as actually was achieved has been consumed by a reduction in working hours, rather than passed through into higher wages, reinforces this picture of slow growth.

There is no doubt that the direct effects of current and planned revenue increases and expenditure cuts are and will be contractionary. The indirect effects, and in particular the consequences for monetary policy, are more difficult to gauge. The Bundesbank has clearly stated that it will condition a further relaxation of monetary policy on a substantial reduction of public sector borrowing, and that this reduction has to be accomplished on the expenditure side. The interest rate effects of the Bundesbank's stance have already been discussed. Even recent analyses hint that the interest rate effects of federal deficits and indebtedness are relatively small;[2] the interest rate reductions that would be needed to balance the contractionary effects of deficit reduction of the magnitude projected here are beyond any reasonable expectation.[3] The experience of 1990 and 1991 indicates that the price effects have been similarly small. Price increases in the Federal Republic stayed within narrow margins and were primarily caused by rising costs. As mentioned above, government-administered prices, social security contributions, and taxes contributed a great deal to this inflation. Wage policy also played a decisive role: the expansive fiscal policy of the early 1990s encouraged wage increases. Moreover, higher taxes quickly translated into higher wage demands.[4]

One also has to consider the immediate normative aspects of deficit reduction, which arise mostly from the decisions made in Maastricht on December 10, 1991, and which have become the central guideline for budget policies in the EU countries. Moreover, budget deficit ceilings postulated in the Basic

Law also require deficit reduction in light of the economic stabilization anticipated by 1995.

Without a doubt, the fiscal picture in the Federal Republic has changed drastically since unification. Since 1991 these changes have led to a number of changes in expenditure and revenue policy (notably the reduction of subsidies and consumption-type expenditures), which are undeniably for the better from the perspective both of prudent public administration and of economic growth. These measures, however, have not been very far-reaching. Moreover, a number of the cost-reduction measures, for example the cuts in research and higher education spending, will have a negative impact on growth. Negative consequences are also to be expected for employment policy, due to the increase in nonwage labor costs caused by the raising of social security contributions to finance unification.[5] In addition, the distributional effects of the consolidation were, until 1994, quite regressive, both from a functional and from an individual perspective, especially if anticipated future wage and labor market developments are considered; this is so notwithstanding the fact that distributional effects should play a subordinate role, given the required investments in both eastern and western Germany. Finally, it should be remembered that the current financial planning of the federal government still carries with it a number of substantial risks.

All these considerations lead one to ask whether there are possible alternative or additional policy strategies available whose adoption would improve the fiscal picture. In principle there are four basic types of strategies for consolidating public budgets or reducing a country's net indebtedness:[6]

- a *"passive" strategy of automatic reduction,* in which policymakers rely on an eventual cyclical upswing in the economy to gain greater latitude in reducing the deficit;
- an *"active" strategy of reduction through expansive economic policy,* in which the deficit is, as in the first strategy, reduced through economic growth, but that growth is actively sought through expansive macroeconomic policies;
- a *strategy of discretionary reduction,* in which the deficit is reduced through an increase in revenues and a reduction of expenditures, without, however, restraining economic growth;
- a *strategy of structural consolidation,* in which the revenue and expenditure structures of the public budgets are adjusted to stimulate economic growth, resulting in higher revenues and lower expenditures.

Obviously, the contribution that each of these strategies can make to deficit reduction has to be evaluated in the light of fiscal policy measures already taken, the fiscal burden that the private sector has to bear, the economy's growthpotential, and other factors. None of these strategies alone would be sufficient to overcome all the country's fiscal problems without serious social, economic, and political repercussions. This conclusion is supported by the simulations on the financing of unification discussed earlier and by the analysis below.

The Federal Republic's experience with budget consolidation in the 1980s also argues for a combination of strategies. Between 1981 and 1989 most deficit reduction was accomplished by discretionary policy measures, but cyclical and growth factors also supported the consolidation effort.[7] Capital transfers decreased by 0.7 percentage point and current transfers by 0.4 percentage point. The share of interest payments, however, tripled, increasing by 0.8 percentage point. Seen from a functional perspective, expenditures on social security, welfare and housing, education, and economic services were cut especially sharply. On the revenue side, the share of income-related taxes in GDP decreased minimally (by 0.1 percentage point), whereas that of consumption taxes dropped significantly (by 0.4 percentage point), probably because of their less than proportional income elasticity. With an increase of 0.6 percentage point, the GDP share of social security contributions rose considerably.

To what extent these developments can be linked to one or more of the four strategies outlined above is not a question that can be answered completely and unambiguously. A final judgment would require consideration of fiscal policy in 1990, which witnessed the last phase of a three-phase tax reduction (the first two were in 1986 and 1988) totaling DM 35 billion (1.3 percent of GDP) and created a growth impulse of 1 percent.[8]

Given the present deficit situation, a strategy of explicit expenditure- or revenue-stimulated increase in growth, of the kind often used to overcome a cyclical downturn, is the least likely to be realized and will not be considered below. Nevertheless, it is worthwhile to ask how much economic growth would be necessary to improve the budget position of the Federal Republic. The following discussion of the remaining three strategies is based on the official budget plan of 1994 (see chapter 2).

A Strategy of Automatic Reduction

With the advent of German unification, a strategy of this kind has to be conceived in regional terms.

EASTERN GERMANY. The transfer needs of the east—the principal determinant of the German deficit—will in turn be determined by expected economic growth in the new Länder and the assistance required there for reconstruction, as well as the need for social cushioning of the restructuring process (through wage compensation and pensions, for example) and specific assistance to bring the standard of living up to western German levels (through provision of public infrastructure, finance administration, and so on). The federal government estimates—and these findings are widely accepted in the German policy community—that the adjustment process will not be completed before the end of this decade and that current gross transfers will have to be kept at the current relative level until 1997.[9]

Among the transfers listed in table 2-13, VAT compensation among the Länder and subsidies to unemployment insurance are particularly growth sensitive. The contributions of the Fund for German Unity are fixed and will be discontinued at the end of 1994. Beginning in 1995, the interest and amortization payments will be covered by the so-called unification-related federal payments (*Einigungsbedingten Ausgaben des Bundes*).

If economic growth in the east should dramatically exceed current forecasts and expectations—which, incidentally, vary widely[10]—the fiscal burden of transfer payments would obviously be greatly reduced. However, to produce an additional annual reduction in the numbers of registered unemployed by 100,000 until 1997, real annual GDP growth of 20 percent would be needed, which in turn would require productivity growth of 11 percent per year (as in the *Prognos* forecast, which the federal government apparently used as its guide), and even then 100 percent of the new jobs created would have to be filled by persons now unemployed (currently the recruitment rate is 30 percent in western Germany).[11] Sustained growth at such a rapid pace over several years is beyond the experience of any industrialized country. Moreover, even if realized, the immediate relief on public budgets would be relatively small: raising eastern German wages and incomes to the levels of those in the west by 1997 would generate additional annual savings of DM 2.8 billion, which would accumulate to DM 56 billion by 1997, disregarding the initial year (1992). Assuming that those then employed would receive salaries equal to those in the west, the government would gain additional revenues of DM 2.3 billion annually in the form of taxes and contributions. These additional revenues, however, would probably not greatly reduce the transfer needs of the east in the period considered here, not to mention the institutional question of how to appropriate these additional revenues. A different scenario emerges if the reduction in unemployment is accomplished by unemployed workers dropping out of the labor force. Here, however, it is an open question to what extent this would cause an increase in social transfers, which in turn would dampen the otherwise positive effect of lower unemployment benefit payments on the public budgets.

The outlook for transfer payments, and thus for the budget as a whole, appears much more optimistic if income and economic policy goals and activities are no longer solely determined by the objective of raising income levels in the east as rapidly as possible. For example, if reducing unemployment took priority as a policy goal, the reduction of transfer needs would be much greater, since unemployment compensation would also drop.[12]

WESTERN GERMANY. The situation in western Germany is quite different: higher rates of growth generate higher tax and social security revenues and reduce expenditures for unemployment benefits. In this study, higher levels of employment are generally associated with higher levels of economic growth, notwithstanding current discussions about alternative solutions through a shortening of working hours (on a weekly, yearly, or lifelong basis). These strategies will not be discussed below. Although they could defuse the employment problem temporarily,[13] they would solve the deficit problem only partially at best. In fact, by increasing social security expenditures they might even worsen the problem. In addition, they do not contribute to the solution of the income problem noted above.

The question of how a path of sustained and rising growth could be realized is not addressed here, not least because it goes far beyond the immediate issues and problems arising from German unification. But it is widely agreed that there is no easy or quick solution.[14] The assumptions used for the growth scenarios discussed in chapter 2 offer few reasons for optimism. Even a decisive devaluation of the deutsche mark vis-à-vis the dollar, accompanied by a considerable reduction in long-term real interest rates and a sustained increase in the volume of world trade, would only increase the average GDP growth rate in Germany by a little over 0.5 percentage point.[15]

A 1 percent increase in real GDP in western Germany creates additional revenues of almost DM 7.5 billion (DM 4 billion from direct taxes and DM 3.5 billion from indirect taxes). This is expected to increase by DM 0.5 billion, to DM 8 billion by 1997, assuming that the present differential between nominal and real growth does not change. Inflationary growth would have few consequences for deficit reduction given that public revenues and expenditures would rise in parallel with nominal GDP.[16] At any rate, the slow growth path assumed here requires a tightening of expenditures in order to achieve the intended deficit reduction.[17]

An increase in western German growth by 1 percent creates additional annual revenues from social security contributions of DM 6.5 billion, and from unemployment insurance contributions of DM 1.3 billion. In other words, a 1 percent increase in economic growth would reduce unemployment by 110,000 people—assuming that on average 25 percent of new jobs are filled from the ranks of the registered unemployed—and, besides the additional revenues, a reduction of expenditures by DM 3.8 billion. To sum up, although additional growth may help to ease the deficit burden, growth of the extent currently in prospect will by no means suffice to solve the deficit problem by itself.

A Strategy of Discretionary Reduction

The present consolidation strategy of the federal government, described in the preceding chapter, is predominantly discretionary, even though the quasi-automatic contribution of hidden taxes of about DM 80 billion per year until 1997 does play an important role. In light of the policy measures that have already been implemented, and those that are envisaged in the medium-term financial plan, the latitude for additional measures on both the revenue and the expenditure side is limited. Besides the institutional rigidities, which preclude sudden changes, it is important to understand that such a strategy—for the macroeconomic or cyclical reasons indicated above—will in the short run cause a decline in growth and thus in revenue for the public sector,[18] unless they can be counterbalanced by fundamental changes in investment and consumption behavior.[19] A complete itemization of all the discretionary possibilities would of course be beyond the scope of this study. The discussion that follows will therefore focus on those alternatives that have been most widely discussed in recent public debate.

On the revenue side there are four possibilities that would go beyond the measures currently being considered: new taxes, broadening of the existing tax base, an increase in tax rates, and more efficient and vigorous tax enforcement. Sales of publicly owned assets would play only a supporting role.

The current debate over the introduction of *new taxes* in the Federal Republic focuses mainly on the so-called eco-tax and the restructuring of the tax system to further environmental objectives. Leaving the institutional and administrative problems aside, the core of the debate revolves around the allocative aspects of such taxes and their sectoral and distributive implications. The fiscal implications of such taxes have been of interest only insofar as revenues derived therefrom would be used to promote ecologically sound production and consumption, or the reduction of general direct or indirect taxes or social security contributions, but not to finance general government activities.[20]

For example, the tax on carbon dioxide emissions suggested by the European Commission would have generated revenues of DM 9 billion in the Federal Republic in 1994.[21] That figure would rise to almost DM 26 billion in the year 2000, notwithstanding the possible behavioral response of economic actors to tax-induced changes in energy prices, which in turn would be likely to affect overall energy consumption as well as the general consumption structure. By 1999, revenues from the carbon dioxide tax would amount to about 0.3 percent of GNP and 1.3 percent of all tax revenues. Again ignoring possible behavioral responses, these shares would increase to 0.6 percent and 2 percent, respectively, by the year 2000.

Implementation of a carbon dioxide tax would raise the tax share of GNP by 1 percentage point in 1994 and by 2 percentage points in the year 2000, unless revenues derived from the new tax were offset by an equivalent reduction of other taxes and contributions, as the European Commission has suggested. Obviously such an offset would neutralize the income effect and reduce considerably the intended substitution effect of the eco-tax. If the tax refunds are in the form of reductions in so-called tangible taxes, such as the income tax, this dynamic would tend to be stronger than if compensation were through reductions in intangible taxes, which in many cases still include the VAT. Moreover, in the case of an overall reduction of income tax, a rather intangible charge via the carbon dioxide tax would be balanced by the easing of a rather tangible tax, which could even lead to an overcompensation of the revenue effect of the eco-tax and neutralize the intended substitution effect of the carbon dioxide tax entirely. From a macroeconomic perspective, compensation for the eco-tax through a reduced income tax could even be expansionary. A reduction in the VAT, proposed by the EC Commission as an alternative to the income tax decrease, would be difficult to implement in the Federal Republic, not least because German rates are already at the lower end of the EU range.

Other fundamental changes in the current tax system, such as a local "net value-added tax"[22] or a tax on capital stock (*Maschinensteuer*), which would replace wage payments as an assessment base for social security contributions and generate higher revenues,[23] are not discussed here. Instead we limit our analysis to existing taxes and other contributions. The latter are usually suggested as an alternative to the business tax or to the employer share of social security contributions, not because of their fiscal effects but because of their allocative and distributional effects.

Consideration of a labor market contribution for civil servants arises from the fact that these workers, unlike other employees, do not currently contribute to unemployment insurance—because, it is argued, they face no labor market risk. Contributions by private sector workers and their employers amount to 6.5 percent of workers' incomes and will provide DM 80 billion in revenues in 1994.[24] An equivalent contribution from civil servants would increase these revenues by about DM 6 billion annually (including the employers' share), or 6 percent in 1994. The nature of this contribution, however, contains serious risks from a constitutional and legal perspective, since it places an additional burden on one group in society without them receiving any benefit from the resulting revenues.

The subsidy reports of the federal government provide the frame of reference for a *broadening of the tax base*. The loss of revenues due to narrowing of the tax base as a result of the tax benefits listed there (which is, incidentally, an incomplete list) is estimated at DM 37.5 billion in 1994.[25] The 10 largest benefits claim almost DM 26 billion (almost 70 percent of the total). These benefits consist primarily of measures to promote home ownership (for income tax reasons) and investments in the new Länder and the former east-west border region (these two benefits alone account for more than DM 10 billion in forgone revenues). Tax benefits for cultural and other contributions in the sales tax claim about DM 3.5 billion. Other tax benefits that traditionally are part of the general tax code are not included. These benefits, such as basic abatement, the child and employee exemption, and the deduction of precautionary disbursements from the tax base, reduce tax revenues by about DM 70 billion, or 25 percent, annually.[26] Benefits in conjunction with the sales tax, such as tax-exempted profits (rents)[27] and the halving of the tax rate for daily consumption goods, are not considered either. Similarly, other benefits accruing from various exemptions or deductions, for example in the area of business, wealth, and inheritance taxes, are not taken into account.

The trade tax, with revenues of DM 42 billion in 1994, has deteriorated into a "big company" tax during the last two decades and today probably affects fewer than one-third of taxable businesses. A broadening of its incidence to all profit-making business could generate substantial additional revenues at the local level.[28] Similar considerations apply *mutatis mutandis* to wealth and inheritance taxes (see below). Unlike in the United States, however, efforts to broaden the tax base in the Federal Republic (possibly linked to a reduction of rates) will at least show positive results in the long term. This assessment is based on Germany's experience with tax reform in 1990, when only a small proportion of the measures suggested by politicians and debated in the public were eventually implemented.[29]

Politically less difficult than broadening the tax base would be an *increase in tax rates*,[30] because such an approach spreads rather than concentrates the pain of higher taxes.[31] On many occasions, lawmakers have fallen back on this alternative as the easiest path to financing unification. The most recent increase in the income tax (a 3.75 percent solidarity surcharge on personal and corporate income taxes in 1991 and 1992, generating DM 11 billion annually[32]), the increase in the VAT (by 1 percentage point on January 1, 1994, providing additional revenues of DM 11 billion annually), the increase in the fuel tax (by 16 pfennigs per liter for gasoline and 7 pfennigs per liter for diesel, generating DM 8.5 billion annually[33]), and the gradual increase in the insurance tax up to the level of the sales tax (providing additional annual revenues of DM 4 billion), are only a few examples.

Whether the proposal to adjust assessed values of real estate to match their actual market values (which is relevant with respect to the wealth and inheritance tax) will also prove politically tolerable remains to be seen. Such a change has generally been perceived as long overdue for allocative and distributional reasons and is currently being considered by Germany's supreme court. A revaluation of assessed values—which are now only one-quarter to one-third of market values—is likely to cause, first, a demand for compensation through a reduction in the assessment rate, which is determined by local communities. Second, it would represent a departure from the German tax structure's traditional minor emphasis on assets- or wealth-based taxes. Revenue from wealth taxes currently amounts to only about DM 20 billion, or 2.5 percent of total taxes collected (table 3-1).

These taxes play a more significant role in other major industrial countries.[34] In Japan, Canada, and the United States, for example, their share of total taxes collected is about four times that in the Federal Republic (in 1990 the figures were 9 percent in Japan and Canada, and 11 percent in the United States; figure 3-1). These higher shares reflect most of all the minor role of indirect taxes in these countries, for example the little utilized value-added tax in Japan and the absence of a general consumption tax in the United States.

Table 3-1. Tax Revenues at All Levels of Government, Ranked by Receipts, 1992

Tax	Millions of DM	Percentage of total receipts	Cumulative percentage
Wages and salaries	247,322	33.81	33.81
Turnover and value-added	197,711	27.03	60.84
Fuel	55,166	7.54	68.38
Trade	44,848	6.13	74.51
Income	41,531	5.68	80.19
Corporate	31,184	4.26	84.45
Tobacco	19,253	2.63	87.08
Motor vehicles	13,317	1.82	88.90
Solidarity surcharge	13,027	1.78	90.68
Capital yields	11,273	1.54	92.22
Real property	10,792	1.47	93.69
Insurance	8,094	1.11	94.80
Customs duties	7,742	1.06	95.86
Net worth	6,750	0.92	96.78
Spirits	5,544	0.76	97.54
Real property transfer	5,137	0.70	98.24
Inheritance	3,030	0.41	98.65
Lottery	2,381	0.33	98.98
Coffee	2,125	0.29	99.27
Beer	1,625	0.22	99.49
Sparkling wine	1,083	0.15	99.64
Fire protection	480	0.07	99.71
Entertainment	357	0.02	99.73
Surcharge on land transfers	307	0.04	99.77
Dogs	250	0.03	99.80
Cultural	214	0.03	99.83
Lamp	200	0.03	99.86
Sugar	183	0.03	99.89
Wagering	111	0.02	99.91
Wagering (sports)	98	0.01	99.92
Tea	59	0.01	99.93
Salt	54	0.01	99.94
I.O.U.	48	0.01	99.95
Cinema	43	0.01	99.96
Hunting and fishing	41	0.01	99.97
Beverages	37	0.01	99.98
Wagering (races)	34	0.01	99.99
Stock exchange sales	30	0.01	100.00
Liquor license	1	0.00	100.00
Total tax revenue	731,482	100.00	100.00

Source: Bundesministerium der Finanzen.

Figure 3-1. Wealth and Transfer Taxes in the Group of Seven Countries as a Share of Tax Revenue, 1965, 1980, and 1991[a]

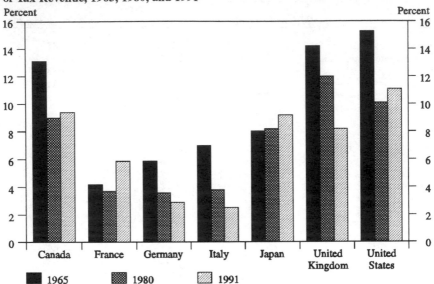

Source: Authors' calculations based on data from OECD.
a. Inheritance, gift, and land transfer taxes.

Among the countries of the European Union, the Federal Republic's share remains considerably below the average of 4.6 percent. An increase to this level would result *ceteris paribus* in additional tax revenues of DM 15 billion annually. An increase to the level of the United States would generate an additional DM 50 billion, but would also raise the share of taxes as a percentage of GNP by 1.5 percentage points, to more than 46 percent—2.5 percentage points above the previous high in the old Federal Republic, reached in 1977. Germany would still rank second among the G-7 countries, after France, but the gap between the two, which was 5 percentage points in 1991 and is likely to narrow to about 3 percentage points by 1994, would be further reduced.

Substantial tax increases beyond the current level would be very problematic for the Federal Republic's international competitive position,[35] whether they are implemented through a broadening of the tax base or by an increase in direct or indirect tax rates.[36] The encouraging signals sent by a lowering of income and corporate tax rates in recent years would come into question. In addition, the efforts of the government to save could be undermined, and the pressure to consolidate the budget through expenditure cuts could be reduced, especially if the government fails to convince investors that the tax increase is of finite duration.

Consolidation achieved primarily through revenue increases—whether implemented openly or through the hidden tax increase (which will amount to DM 80 billion between 1990 and 1997)—is thus likely to affect Germany's international competitiveness. This holds true even if the connections to other financial and macroeconomic parameters are considered, such as the specificity of the tax structure, the government's responsibilities and expenditures given the country's changed priorities, total government indebtedness, western Germany's traditionally strong competitive position owing to its well-qualified human capital, a highly developed material and nonmaterial infrastructure, and a high degree of social consensus.[37]

Apparently, the positive balance between the costs and the benefits of government activity in the old Länder (the *fiscal residuum*) would be considerably smaller, if indeed it did not turn negative. Whether this development would be offset by a rising fiscal residuum in the new Länder through, for example, continuous improvements in infrastructure, remains to be seen. The answer would primarily depend on the structure of public expenditures in the east—that is, whether the funds are used for growth-oriented investment or consumption. In light of western Germany's growth problems, the role of Germany's localization factors is becoming increasingly important.

Germany's ability to pursue a strategy of *stricter tax enforcement*, both from a legislative and an administrative perspective, is relatively limited considering the high degree of international capital mobility. This limitation applies not only to capital gains, which have already to some degree evaded taxation in recent years by fleeing to foreign tax havens,[38] but also to other unofficial and informal tax-relevant activities, which are assumed to generate an estimated DM 150 billion annual loss for the federal government.[39] Moreover, it is questionable to what extent such calculations are realistic, and whether these taxes can and should actually be collected.[40] For example, the calculations often disregard the fact that reducing these tax niches would in all probability reduce the activities themselves, leading thus to lower than anticipated tax revenues. In addition, stricter tax enforcement would create higher compliance costs.[41] Nevertheless, tax enforcement is currently being discussed at the political level. In the fall of 1993 the federal government passed a "Law for the Fight Against Abuse and the Reorganization of the Tax Law." This legislation is expected to collect additional revenues of DM 0.3 billion in 1994, which would increase to DM 2.7 billion by 1997.[42]

Figure 3-2. Public Sector Share of GNP Under Alternative Time Horizons and Rates of Expenditure Increase[a]

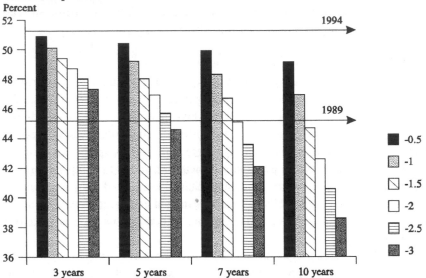

Source: Authors' calculations.
a. Time horizons are indicated on the horizontal axis; rates of expenditure increase are expressed in percentage-point differences from GNP growth (see key at right). For example, keeping expenditures at 1.5 percentage points below GNP growth for seven years would lower the public sector share of GNP to about 47 percent. Arrowed lines indicate actual shares for the years indicated.

reduced, without special allocative or distributive priorities, to such an extent that they grow considerably more slowly than GNP. This would result in a quasi-automatic reduction of the public sector share of GNP.

In this strategy of *general saving*, maintaining expenditure increases, as in the 1980s, at 1.5 percentage points below the 3.5 percent GNP growth rate would lead to a public sector share of GNP of about 47 percent until the year 2000—well short of the 45 percent goal (figure 3-2). With government expenditures at DM 1.67 trillion in 1994, the cuts would yield annual savings of DM 25 billion. Assuming no change in the structure of outlays, about 50 percent would be allocated to government transfers and 38 percent to government consumption. To meet the 45 percent goal by the year 2000, annual public expenditure increases would have to be kept about 2 percentage points below GNP growth, yielding savings of DM 33 billion. The various options are illustrated in figure 3-2.

The alternative strategy is one modeled on "Operation '82" (see chapter 2) and the Employment Initiative of the early 1980s, and the more recent savings through the Federal Consolidation Program (FKP) and the Savings, Consolidation, and Growth Program (SKWP; see the appendix). In such a strategy, government expenditures in specific categories would be reduced. For cxample, personnel compensation and government purchases or transfers, such as some social security benefits and other payments to private households and businesses, could be tightened in a discretionary fashion. It remains to be seen, however, whether this strategy would lead to continuous, year-after-year savings, mostly because the latitude for cuts in this area is limited. After all, taken together the FKP and the SKWP already represent the second-largest fiscal intervention in the history of the Federal Republic, following "Operation '82" and the Employmcnt Initiative. Moreover, it is not clear to what degree additional cuts are politically sustainable.[54]

Thc discretionary reduction of government expenditurcs—the second strategy—would, first of all, have to identify the specific categories whcrc savings could be realized. The possibilities range from public transfers to private households (social transfers) and businesses (subsidies) to all categories of government consumption, which together account for almost nine-tenths of government expenditures. Interest payments on the debt, which in 1994 amounted to more than DM 120 billion (7 percent of the total) are not considered here, because any appreciable discretionary savings in this category seem unlikely.[55]

The second step of the strategy would be to determine which categories should be spared from cuts because of their role in promoting competitiveness and economic growth. Once this has been done, all public sector outlays designed to alter the market-generated income distribution should be the first candidates for cuts. One should distinguish betwccn interpersonal and intergenerational redistributivc mcasures, and betweeu government expenditures that are financed by general tax revenues and those financed by the same group that is ultimatcly their beneficiary. In the area of interpersonal transfers, subsidies to businesses and households, such as housing, child benefits, pension support, and measures to promote private savings, amounted to DM 400 billion in 1994. These should be considered for cuts before contributions-financed services, such as pension and health insurance and unemployment benefits, which together account for two-thirds of public transfers to the private sector.[56] According to the government's medium-term fiscal planning, the latter transfers will have reached an overall level of DM 470 billion by 1997.

No cuts should be made in interpersonal transfers that would worsen the quality of locations for production and the work force. In general, this maxim applies to all investment as well as all consumption-type government expenditures in infrastructure-relevant areas such as education and research, transportation and communication, and, increasingly, living conditions and environmental protection. The extent to which expenditures in traditional budget categories such as government administration, preventive health care, and national security (internal and external) could be reduced needs to be examined on a case-by-case basis. But in all of these areas it will be necessary to explore possibilities for rationalization and greater efficiency.[57]

Public sector personnel compensation, which in 1994 amounted to DM 320 billion, or 50 percent of government consumption and 20 percent of total spending, is one such area. As the following example demonstrates, a tight personnel and wage policy could contribute decisively to relieving government personnel budgets, and state and local personnel budgets most of all.

State and local governments paid the salaries of almost three-fourths (72 percent) of Germany's 5.1 million full-time public servants in 1991. If public sector wages grew each year by 0.5 percent less than those in the private sector until the year 2000 (as happened between 1982 and 1989), DM 1.5 billion per year would be saved. The Länder and local communities would realize DM 1 billion of these savings, and the federal government the rest. If these savings were accompanied by work force cuts of 0.4 percent, or 20,000 employees, per year until the year 2000 (as was also achieved between 1982 to 1989), personnel compensation would decline by another DM 1.5 billion.

Overall, then, savings in personnel compensation of about DM 3 billion annually, or 2 percent of total government expenditures, are not unrealistic, although the secondary income effects would lead to lower tax revenues, which would be likely to reduce the savings to about DM 2 billion, at least in the short run. Leaving these secondary effects aside, public work force reductions of this magnitude would reduce the public sector share of GNP by 0.5 percentage point, to 46 percent by the year 2000, assuming that all other government expenditures grow at a rate 2 percentage points below GNP (figure 3-2). In other words, a restrictive wage and employment policy would reduce the public sector's use of economic resources only in the long term.

In the area of government transfers to the private sector (businesses and households), it is important, first of all, to consider that the public sector spends more than DM 170 billion annually, or 5 percent of GNP—including DM 40 billion in the new Länder—on financial support and tax benefits (subsidies). Clearly, this part of the budget offers many opportunities for expenditure cuts. Yet it must be remembered that the economic consequences of these cuts would be highly concentrated, both regionally and sectorally (with coal mining, farming, shipbuilding, and housing being especially hard hit). Given the labor market and sociopolitical implications of such cuts (not to mention the considerable budgetary consequences of higher expenditures for unemployment benefits or reduced tax revenues), the potential for savings in this area seems limited as well. Nonetheless, if the government were able to implement the same restrictive and incremental policy as it did in the 1980s, annual savings from this source would amount to DM 3.5 billion.[58]

Almost two-thirds (DM 590 billion out of DM 820 billion in 1994) of government transfers to private households are paid by the *parafisci* to cover the broad social risk categories of age, disability, illness, and unemployment. This safety net is financed almost entirely (90 percent) by contributions from employees and employers. The extent to which redistributive elements in individual categories of social insurance can be reduced must be examined in detail. Current estimates indicate that about one-third, or DM 180 billion (5 percent of GNP), of the social insurance budget goes to non-insurance-related activities. This offers the potential for considerable savings. The degree to which they can be realized is an open question, however, especially considering that social security benefits (whether they are matched by contributions or not) are essential to maintaining the standard of living of the elderly. Reductions in these benefits cannot become part of the legislative agenda, not least because they are a central element of Germany's social market economy and thus its notion of a welfare state, which is guaranteed by the constitution. In addition, the benefits arising from the social security system, especially those of mandatory health and unemployment insurance, are a vital element in keeping the social peace between management and labor, and thus also contribute to Germany's attractiveness as a business location. Nevertheless, given the tight fiscal situation, all benefits must be reexamined on an ongoing basis to ensure their efficiency. In 1994 expenditures in these areas added up to DM 640 billion—40 percent of government expenditures and 20 percent of GNP—and are expected to rise to DM 725 billion by 1997.

In sum, the most promising strategy to reduce the deficit seems to be one that reduces expenditures across the board, cutting the public sector share in GNP by increasing public services and expenditures at a rate slower than that of GNP growth. However, to achieve the targeted reduction in the public sector share of GNP will require that, over the next several years, growth in government expenditures be held to a rate more than 2.5 percentage points below GNP. Few seem to have acknowledged the financial and economic impact such a retrenchment would have, especially considering that the fiscal policy challenges in eastern Germany demand that many expenditures in western Germany remain stagnant in real and in some cases even in nominal terms.

IV. Conclusion

In this chapter we indicate several possible revisions to current revenue and expenditure planning in Germany, including some relating to the adoption of less ambitious deficit goals. First, however, it is appropriate to define the boundaries we have set for ourselves in this discussion. The political and institutional prerequisites, such as those addressed by Wagner's Law, Peacock and Wiseman's displacement and plateau theory, and Baumol's concept of unbalanced productivity growth,[1] are not discussed here, nor do we take into account Baumol's writings on included determinants, such as the stability and polarity of the political system, consensus among political decision makers, and ideological differences among political parties.[2] The same applies to the question of the extent to which the proposed policy measures can be implemented at the different levels of government. Despite the presence of various coordinating bodies, such as fiscal planning councils and state finance ministers' conferences, and despite the dominant importance of the federal government, which absorbs one-fourth of total government expenditures, and two-fifths of those of all territorial (federal, state, and local) authorities, there are considerable risks involved, especially at the state level.[3] Finally, the discussion is couched in general terms, given our still limited knowledge about the how and why of the budget process and its decision making. It also abstains from formulating any strategic goals, which are usually part of medium-term fiscal planning.[4]

Any further consideration of concrete expenditure and revenue policy measures needs to be addressed in light of four developments. First, the Federal Republic will be required to continue the annual transfer of about 5 percent of western German GNP to the east from now until the end of the decade. Despite this heavy burden, Germany is likely to reduce the share of its public deficit in GNP by more than half by the end of 1997, and thus meet the Maastricht criterion of 3 percent. The debt-GNP ratio will exceed the Maastricht criterion for this measure (60 percent) by 1 percentage point in 1995 but is expected to decrease to about 55 percent by 1997.

Second, the Federal Republic will face historically high tax rates at least until 1997. This has led to a situation where the international environment increasingly serves as a constraint on policy action. These high rates can no longer find justification by reference to the qualitative equivalence of public and private expenditures.

Third, although most of the initial bias against employees and lower income groups in shouldering the financial burden of German unification will be mitigated through revisions in tax policy, in particular through the solidarity surcharge, the rather somber outlook for growth and productivity will make the overall burden feel particularly heavy on those groups. On average, Germans should not expect any tangible increase in real net income for the next few years. Moreover, many Germans will feel the regressive effects of a tight expenditure policy.[5]

Finally, in western Germany this policy will cause not just real but even nominal expenditure reductions, whose structural effects (i.e., the reduction of investment) will constrain economic growth. Fiscal planning needs to take these factors into account, yet none of them seem to be widely recognized in current fiscal planning.

For the foreseeable future, the core of Germany's fiscal policy should be strengthening and sustaining economic growth. Such a strategy not only improves the fiscal picture but increases the capacity of the economy to cope with the tax burden. Given the primacy of economic growth, Germany's policy options are quite limited: the (partial) reimbursement of hidden tax increases and less reliance on social security contributions to finance unification in order to maintain the high degree of social consensus in the Federal Republic.[6]

Given the macroeconomic forecasts and the current budgetary situation, the medium-term fiscal plan of the federal, state, and local governments more or less exhausts the existing policy options. Although realism has dominated current fiscal planning, politicians have not succeeded in sufficiently emphasizing both the importance of continued growth and the government's lack of adequate finances. The latter has been done only for health care, social policy, and defense. While businesses have long been cognizant of the lean times ahead,[7] households are only slowly becoming aware of this reality. A successful fiscal policy will thus also depend on the ability of policymakers to generate greater public awareness of these circumstances. This includes an understanding that even discretionary policies have limited applicability. The need for greater awareness of Germany's current fiscal situation also applies to the European and the broader international environment, where the Federal Republic's limited fiscal strength is not yet universally recognized.[8] As to the deficit sensitivity of the budget, the second element of structural consolidation, the verdict is less unequivocal. Whereas the greater share of income taxes in total taxes increases the cyclical sensitivity of the budget, the reductions in social transfer payments have the opposite effect. On balance, deficit sensitivity seems to have increased.

Policy Options

Future policy should emphasize structural consolidation, aiming at increasing productivity and growth and, if possible without compromising these goals, seeking to reduce the deficit sensitivity of the budget. On the revenue side this means a restructuring of the tax code so as to lower personal taxes, including social security contributions. On the expenditure side it means a regrouping in favor of expenditures that promote growth. Additional revenues should be used to support this policy.

REVENUES. On the assumption that the tax burden should not be increased, additional policy measures to increase revenues play a subordinate role. It is true that minor revenue improvements are possible, for example through updating the assessed value of housing or limiting tax benefits in this area, through stricter tax enforcement, or through an increase in property and wealth taxes. But the resulting additional revenues would not exceed DM 30 billion annually, or 1 percent of current tax revenues, barring reform of the entire tax code.

Given the already high level of taxation, any such additional tax revenue should be used to reduce social security contributions, to the extent that these are used to finance unification, rather than cut direct taxes, including the solidarity surcharge (which is not bound by any time limit); a reduction of social security contributions is desirable not only from a labor market and competitiveness perspective (to reduce nonwage labor costs), but also from a distributional policy perspective. This policy should be pursued despite the fact that Germans can expect further increases in hidden taxes and that the current share of direct taxes in total tax revenue (48 percent), which includes the solidarity surcharge, has not reached the historic high (50 percent) experienced in the mid-1970s and 1980s.

In addition, it would help matters if policymakers publicly announced that tax rates will be reduced in the medium term.[9] A case in point is the solidarity surcharge, which goes into effect on January 1, 1995.[10] Arguments against such a public statement, pointing to the experience of the mid-1970s and in particular that of 1990-91, are not very convincing.[11] Much greater caution should be exercised in proposing actual tax reductions, whether they are made with the intention of disciplining public expenditures,[12] in anticipation of higher revenues, or by pointing to their self-financing character, as supply-side advocates sometimes do. Although some self-financing will occur, it will not be the result of a supply-side-generated increase in economic growth (as previously mentioned), but rather of demand-side effects. In any case, the current fiscal situation has enough disciplinary implications and does not need any additional incentives. At the same time, however, there is no need to "hoard" any means for future tax reductions. Indeed, a *Zug um Zug* approach is the most appropriate.[13]

EXPENDITURES. In the search for additional elements of a growth-oriented fiscal consolidation, expenditures take on a more important role than revenues. In this context the substitutive elements of private sector activities have so far been at the center of the public debate. The complementary aspects have received less attention, and in some cases have even been ignored. For example, few have criticized or even noticed the fact that current fiscal planning calls for expenditure increases at 2 percentage points *below* the rate of economic growth. Given the extensive expenditure reviews in the wake of the change of government in 1982, as well as since 1992, the scope for further cuts to meet this target are rather slim.

Certainly one important category is public sector wages and salaries. But given the cuts and rationalizations that have already taken place, the additional savings from belt tightening here would not be very large. Continued pressure in the labor market will reduce the opportunities for a disproportionate wage increase, although structural improvements will be necessary to meet the demand for labor in such growing areas as tax administration, police, and the environment. To compensate, it will be necessary to further improve efficiency in the public sector, and additional privatization of public services can no longer be excluded. The total potential savings in this category run between DM 1 billion and DM 2 billion.

Additional room for cuts can be found in programs that support the construction of housing and household saving, as well as in the area of subsidies. Since such measures cannot be implemented retroactively, however, savings over the next few years will not exceed DM 5 billion annually or, *ceteris paribus*, 0.2 percentage point of the public sector share in GNP.

Considering the rather depressed medium-term economic outlook for western Germany, one may wonder whether the current plan should not contain expenditure *increases* rather than cuts in such categories as research and development and education. Merely expanding these categories at the same rate as current GNP would require additional expenditures of DM 6 billion annually.[14] An alternative possibility that is certainly worth exploring is to determine whether the same effects could not be achieved more cost-effectively on the revenue side, such as through a fee-for-service principle. However, the potential improvements in efficiency resulting from such an approach should be measured against any negative distributional implications, the weakening of the meritocratic nature of these areas, and the reduction of positive externalities.

The Deficit: Policy Means or End?

To conclude, a growth-oriented fiscal policy must also examine the question of the correct size of the deficit, most importantly because of its depletion of private sector savings, even though this relationship has been weakened by increased international capital mobility.

The deficit reduction currently projected in the government's medium-term financial plan is exceptionally swift and intense relative to Germany's own past experience as well as to international standards. Even if the government's goal of a deficit share of GNP of 2 percent by 1997 were relaxed to 3 percent, the Maastricht criteria would still be met. At the same time, such a relaxation would give policymakers an additional DM 35 billion with which to adjust policies on both the income and the expenditure side. This amount is roughly equivalent to what could be raised through additional revenues and far exceeds the amount that could be raised by additional expenditure cuts. At the same time, it is very likely that if the suggested income and expenditure policy measures are used to stimulate growth, an even sharper reduction of the deficit would be possible by the end of the time period considered in this study. By 1997 the deficit could be reduced to less than 2.5 percent of GNP.

Finally, leaving aside any fiscal-strategic aspects, when evaluating various deficit goals the following two considerations deserve special attention. First, the German economy is of central importance to the economies of other European countries, and thus also to their fiscal situation: 1-percentage-point faster growth in Germany leads to 0.2 percent faster growth and an additional DM 6 billion in revenues in the European Union as a whole. There are a number of good reasons not to let the level of taxation surpass its current levels. National and international circumstances also lead to the conclusion that the overall goal of economic growth must be considered to a much greater extent than in the past when contemplating further expenditure cuts.[15] This would help Germany, Europe, and the international community more than clinging to a deficit goal at all costs. After all, a settlement of the Debt Redemption Fund would reduce the deficit by DM 25 billion (0.7 percentage point) and the debt by DM 400 billion (12 percentage points).

We do not in any way mean to downplay what is indeed a very serious problem. The necessary structural consolidation requires a much more ardent and consistent effort on the part of economic and fiscal policymakers than has been demonstrated thus far—indeed more than has ever been necessary in the history of the Federal Republic. But any attempt at consolidation should keep the instrumental role of the deficit in mind and not lose sight of the rather arbitrary formulation of the deficit and debt ratios in the Maastricht criteria. However confidently and adroitly Germany's politicians handle unification and its attendant fiscal challenges, Germans face a period of economic development that is below their expectations—and certainly below the country's possibilities. But on the other hand, the distresses to be encountered, when measured against the resources available to bear them, fall well short of tragic proportions.

Appendix: Chronology of the Fiscal Policy Measures of German Unification

1990

January 1 A foreign travel currency fund comes into force, enabling East German citizens to acquire deutsche marks in exchange for East German marks: DM 100 may be exchanged at a rate of one to one, and a further DM 100 at a rate of one to five, per calendar year. The Federal Republic pays up to DM 2.15 billion into this fund, and East Germany DM 0.75 billion. This replaces the *Begrüßungsgeld* (a cash payment given to East Germans on crossing the border) of DM 100.

March 30 The Bundestag (the lower house of the West German legislature) passes a supplement to the 1990 federal budget: the total budget is set at DM 306.9 billion, DM 6.8 billion higher than originally passed. The additional funds are intended primarily (DM 5.8 billion of the total supplement) to provide economic and humanitarian emergency aid to East Germany. Of this sum, DM 4.0 billion is designated for immediate direct payments to East Germany, and DM 1.8 billion for payments to East Germans in the Federal Republic. The net credit loan is estimated at DM 32.9 billion.

May 18 The first state treaty between the Federal Republic and the GermanDemocratic Republic is signed by ministers of finance Theo Waigel and Walter Romberg. Prior to this the draft contract for the creation of Monetary, Economic, and Social Union had been approved by the cabinets in Bonn and East Berlin. The Federal Republic approves a draft bill establishing the German Unity Fund (Fonds Deutsche Einheit) and a second supplementary budget for 1990. In the German Unity Fund the Federal Republic commits itself to partly alleviate the deficits in the East German national budget arising during the transition from a centrally planned economy to a market economy. The costs of financing are to be borne by the federation, the Länder (states), and local communities through the German Unity Fund. Out of this fund, East Germany is to receive a total of DM 115 billion over the next four and one half years: DM 22 billion in 1990, DM 35 billion in 1991, DM 28 billion in 1992, DM 20 billion in 1993, and DM 10 billion in 1994. Of the total DM 115 billion, DM 20 billion is to be financed through reductions in costs related to maintaining and defending the border, and DM 95 billion through credit loans. The federal government and the governments of the Länder each contribute half to the annuity (10 percent).

For the fund, the federal and state governments must defray the following expenditures over the next few years (in billions of deutsche marks):

Year	Federal government	Länder
1990	2.0	0.0
1991	5.0	1.0
1992	6.6	2.6
1993	8.8	3.8
1994	9.5	4.5

The federal and state governments agree that the current costs of German division, in particular the tax incentives in accordance with the Berlin assistance law and the *Zonenrandförderung* (financial assistance to the regions along the internal border) will be abolished within seven years. The federal government agrees to issue detailed proposals for further expenditure cuts.

The second supplementary budget for 1990 is set at DM 311.7 billion, DM 4.8 billion more than the first supplementary budget. DM 2.75 billion is earmarked for the initial financing of pension and unemployment insurance in East Germany. DM 2 billion goes to the German Unity Fund. The higher expenditures are more than offset by a growth-induced surplus of tax receipts, and the net credit loan is reduced to DM 30.9 billion, DM 2 billion less than originally planned.

June 21 To carry out the conversion of East German marks into deutsche marks, East Germany agrees to establish an equalization fund. Beginning on July 1, 1990, interest-bearing claims will be allocated to banks and foreign trade operations in East Germany against the equalization fund when capital does not cover obligations because of the currency conversion. The interest rate on these claims is to correspond to the supply rate for money market shares in banks in Frankfurt (the Frankfurt interbank offer rate, or FIBOR) for a time period corresponding to the interest period (three months).

East Germany agrees to create a pension, health, accident, and unemployment insurance plan in accordance with Federal Republic regulations. Pension, health, and accident insurance will be handled by a common authority at first; by 1991 the new plan is to become part of the federal system.

East Germany will also introduce a social assistance system corresponding to that in the Federal Republic. To overcome the financial bottlenecks that are expected to follow the change, the Federal Republic accords East Germany certain financial allocations: an estimated DM 22 billion for the second half of 1990 and DM 35 billion for 1991. Budget assistance for deferred financing of social insurance is planned; this is set at DM 2.75 billion for 1990 and DM 3 billion for 1991. East Germany's credit authorization is limited to DM 10 billion for 1990 and DM 14 billion for 1991; the Federal Republic's minister of finance may allow the credit limit to be exceeded under fundamentally changed circumstances.

June 22 The Bundestag passes the second supplement to the 1990 federal budget: the amount is set at DM 311.8 billion, and the net credit loan is estimated at DM 31 billion.

July 3 The federal government adopts a draft for the federal budget for 1991 and a medium-term financial plan through 1994.

Compared with the debt established in the second supplementary budget of 1990 in the 1991 budget, federal expenditure will rise by 3.9 percent to DM 324 billion. The net credit loan is set at DM 31.3 billion, DM 0.3 billion higher than in the second supplementary budget.

In financial planning through 1994, increases in federal expenditures for 1992 through 1994 of 3 percent are expected; the net credit loan is set at DM 24 billion for 1992, DM 17.5 billion for 1993, and DM 11.6 billion for 1994.

July 22 The East German parliament passes its DM 64.2 billion budget with a DM 32 billion deficit (DM 22 billion of which is financed by the German Unity Fund).

August 30 Minister of Finance Waigel announces the third supplement to the 1990 federal budget. DM 20 billion will go to offset the deficits in the East German social insurance scheme. The cabinet is scheduled to vote on the supplement on October 4, the federal parliament on October 24, and the federal council on October 26.

August 31 West German Minister of the Interior Wolfgang Schäuble and East German Secretary of State Günter Krause sign the Second State Treaty "concerning the restoration of the unity of Germany" —the Unification Treaty. Parliamentary ratification is expected by the end of September.

The Unification Treaty creates the basis for the merging of the two German states: as of October 3, the national, legal, and economic order of the Federal Republic will apply in most respects to East Germany as well. The Unification Treaty transfers the judicial system of the Federal Republic to the five yet-to-be-established Länder in East Germany; the various exceptions and reservations allowed by the treaty are limited in time. This applies also to regulations that concern the financial constitution.

Proceeds from the sales tax will be apportioned into an eastern and a western share. In 1991 the eastern German Länder should receive an average sales tax share of 55 percent of the average share of residents of western Germany. This share should rise to 70 percent by 1994, and from 1995 on the two shares should be the same.

Special measures to stimulate the eastern German economy include:

—DM 10 billion for loans at subsidized interest rates for local community investments, which will reduce the interest rate by up to 10 percent over ten years;

—DM 10 billion for preferred loans to modernize housing, with a maximum of DM 10,000 per applicant;

—a 23 percent investment subsidy, structured according to the framework of the western German system of regional assistance;

—the expected costs of DM 3 billion a year are to be met by the federal government and the new Länder;

—up to 85 percent of the money in the German Unity Fund will be allocated to the eastern German Länder; the remaining 15 percent will be allocated to the federation to fulfill national tasks in eastern Germany.

September 10 The Federal Republic and the Soviet Union agree that the former will contribute DM 12 billion toward the withdrawal of Soviet troops from eastern Germany.

October 5 The federal cabinet approves the third supplementary budget with an additional volume of DM 20 billion.

October 9 The Federal Republic and the Soviet Union reach final agreement on the withdrawal of Soviet troops from the territory of the former East Germany. Of the DM 12 billion that the Federal Republic will transfer to the Soviet Union for relocation expenses, DM 7.8 billion will go to finance a housing program for returning soldiers in 1991 and 1992; DM 1 billion will defray the costs of stationing the troops in 1990 and 1991; DM 1 billion will help relocate troops; and DM 0.2 billion will help with education and retraining.

October 25 The parliament of the Federal Republic approves the third supplementary budget. Besides changes affecting the western German territory, the budget includes the budget of the former East Germany from July 22, 1990. The net deficit is DM 25 billion higher than previously planned because of lower revenues and higher expenditures in eastern Germany.

November 14 The federal government announces that it will limit increases in government spending from 1991 to 1994 to 2 percent a year, to limit the net deficit in 1991 to DM 70 billion, and to lower it by 1994 to DM 30 billion. The necessary reallocations are to be DM 35 billion in 1991 and DM 70 billion in 1994.

1991

January 1 Old age pensions in eastern Germany are increased by 15 percent.

January 10 The government provides details on the DM 35 billion deficit reduction scheduled for 1991. Revenues are to be increased by raising various contributions (DM 20.3 billion), privatizing government holdings (DM 0.5 billion), and by various savings (DM 14.2 billion). The unemployment insurance contribution rate is to increase by 1.5 percent. The contribution rate to the old age pension fund will be lowered by 1 percent. Expected net revenues from these measures are DM 18.3 billion. A special surcharge of the federal post office in 1991 94 is expected to yield DM 2 billion each year.

Defense expenditures are to be reduced by DM 7.6 billion, and tax privileges for Berlin and the former intra-German border regions are to be cut by DM 1.5 billion. The expenditures of the Federal Employment Agency (Bundesanstalt für Arbeit) are to be reduced by DM 2.3 billion and fiscal aid by DM 1 billion. Postponing certain government investments will cut DM 2.3 billion.

February 20 The federal government agrees on a budget for 1991 with total expenditures of DM 399.7 billion and a net deficit of DM 69.5 billion. According to financial planning through 1994, expenditures in 1992 are to be limited to a 0.8 percent increase, and in 1993 and 1994 to 2.2 percent. Net credits are to be restricted to DM 49.4 billion in 1992, DM 40.6 billion in 1993, and DM 30.9 billion in 1994.

February 28 At a conference between state ministers and Chancellor Helmut Kohl, the federal government resolves to improve the financial situation in eastern Germany with the allocation of approximately DM 22 billion:

—The federal government grants the new Länder additional aid of DM 5 billion for investment in cities, counties, and communities. These funds are to be distributed according to population.

—The federal government relinquishes its portion of the German Unity Fund and offers an additional DM 7 billion to the new Länder to promote investment and employment.

—Instead of following the step-by-step plan laid out in the Unification Treaty, the new Länder will as of January 1, 1991, benefit from the revenue tax in proportion to their populations.

March 8 The federal government creates the Gemeinschaftswerk Aufschwung Ost (Partnership for Eastern Renewal) by levying a 7.5 percent surcharge on income and corporate taxes payable between July 1, 1991, and June 30, 1992, and by permanently increasing taxes on mineral oil products, insurance, and tobacco. Part of the revenue is to be used to:

—improve local infrastructure, in particular to modernize hospitals and homes for the elderly (DM 5 billion in outlays in 1991);

—speed up vocational training as well as establish new enterprises(DM 2.5 billion in 1991, DM 3 billion in 1992);

—accelerate improvements in transportation infrastructure (DM 1.4 billion in 1991, DM 4.2 billion in 1992);

—extend the deadlines for increased investment subsidies to the end of 1991 92 and allow them to be combined with special depreciation allowances (DM 0.4 billion in 1991, DM 0.65 billion in 1992);

—concentrate regional assistance for job creation programs in depressed areas (DM 0.6 billion in 1991 and 1992);

—assist the adjustment process in the shipbuilding industry (DM 0.13 billion in 1991, DM 0.4 billion in 1992);

—provide emergency assistance for the environment (DM 0.4 billion in 1991 and 1992);

—modernize university buildings and student housing (DM 0.2 billion in 1991 and 1992);

—renovate federal buildings (DM 0.27 billion in 1991, DM 0.05 billion in 1992).

May 14 The Bundestag extends the special regulations for payments to short-term workers in the new Länder beyond December 31, 1991. The special regulations for job-creating activities in these states are extended beyond 1992. The age limit for certain pension claims is reduced from 57 years to 55 years.

June 7 The Bundestag approves the budget for 1992, with an 8 percent increase over the 1990 budget and its three supplements. Proposed net expenditures for 1991 amount to DM 66.4 billion.

June 17 The federal government plans to increase the value-added tax (VAT) in 1993 and to lower corporate taxes.

July 1 Old age pensions in eastern Germany are increased by 15 percent. Laws increasing taxes on income, gasoline, insurance, and tobacco come into effect, with estimated revenues for 1991 of DM 17.4 billion, and for 1992 of DM 26.8 billion. Various taxes in eastern Germany are reduced (including through special depreciation rates and a cut in income tax rates) this is estimated to decrease revenues in 1991 by DM 2.5 billion, and in 1992 by DM 3.4 billion.

July 10 The federal government agrees on the 1992 federal budget and on a financial plan through 1995. Expenditures are expected to rise by 3 percent from those in the 1991 budget plan, amounting to DM 422.6 billion. The net deficit will shrink by DM 15.2 billion. In 1993 expenditures are expected to increase by 1.4 percent, and in 1994 and 1995 by 2.4 percent. Net credits are to be reduced to DM 64 billion in 1993, DM 30.2 billion in 1994, and DM 25.1 billion in 1995.

September 2 The federal government agrees on a draft bill to relieve the income tax burden on families and companies by 1992. It will be offset by an increase in the VAT from 14 to 15 percent and by reducing tax exemptions. The federal government decides to repeal DM 2.45 billion in structural aid for the Länder by 1992 and to increase its contribution to the German Unity Fund by a corresponding amount through 1994. In addition, the federal government will increase its contribution by DM 3.45 billion in 1992, and by DM 1 billion in 1993 and 1994, to improve the fiscal situation of the new Länder.

October 17 The federal government decides on a second budget for 1991 to meet the additional DM 5 billion in unemployment-related expenditures of the Federal Employment Office in 1992; the amount is to be financed mainly by expenditure savings in other areas in 1991.

November 29 The Bundestag agrees on a budget for 1992, with an increase in spending over 1991 levels of 2.9 percent. Planned expenditures amount to DM 422.1 billion, with a net deficit of DM 45.3 billion.

   The Bundesrat (the upper house of the federal legislature) rejects the tax reform law of 1992 and the Structural Assistance Amendment Law (*Strukturhilfe-änderungsgesetz*).

December 11 The federal government accords the Treuhandanstalt a maximum credit limit of DM 30 billion for 1992 94, but under certain conditions this may be extended by DM 8 billion.

December 12 The federal government decides to extend transition payments to the elderly in the new Länder by six months, to June 30, 1992.

1992

January 1 The pension law of the Federal Republic is introduced into the new Länder, and a financial alliance between the eastern and western old age pension insurance systems is created.

February 14 The Bundesrat passes the Tax Amendment Law of 1992 (*Steueränderungsgesetz 1992*) as well as the Law to Amend the Structural Assistance Law and Supplement the German Unity Fund (*Gesetz zur Aufhebung des Strukturhilfegesetzes und zur Aufstockung des Fonds 'Deutsche Einheit'*) in a compromise version suggested by the arbitrators. Their provisions include the following:

—The annual DM 2.45 billion in federal structural aids formerly transferred to the old Länder will be used to increase the German Unity Fund and thus to help the new Länder. In addition, the federal share of this fund is increased by DM 3.45 billion to improve the fiscal situation of the eastern German Länder and local communities. Additional federal revenues from the increase in the VAT from 14 to 15 percent (the lower rate for basic goods is left unchanged) in 1993 and 1994 will be used to support the German Unity Fund.

—The share of the Länder in VAT revenues from the turnover tax will increase from 35 percent to 37 percent.

—The newly implemented tax program that eases the financial burden on families will be extended. The *Erstkindergeld* (financial assistance for each family's firstborn dependent child) is increased from DM 50 to DM 70 per month (an additional expenditure of DM 2.4 billion). Low-income families are to receive an increase in allowances from DM 48 to DM 65 per month (an additional expenditure of DM 0.7 billion), and income tax exemptions per child are to be raised from DM 3,024 to DM 4,104 (a decrease in revenue in 1992 of DM 3.2 billion and in 1993 of DM 3.8 billion).

The tax structure is to be improved in 1993. Among other reforms, the net worth tax for companies is to be decreased and simplified, and the business yields tax is to be raised and refined (a decrease in revenue of DM 4.5 billion).

—Additional tax incentives for real estate investment, including exemptions for housing investment loans, will be created over the next four years in accordance with the income tax law.

May 13 The federal government decides on a draft supplementary budget for 1992 and on goals for medium-term financial policy.

In the supplementary budget for 1992, expenditures, mainly to finance further investment incentives in the new Länder, are planned to total DM 426 billion— DM 3.9 billion more than in the previous budget plan. The net deficit is estimated at DM 42.7 billion, DM 2.6 billion less than in the previous estimate, as a result of cutbacks and higher tax revenues. According to the medium-term financial policy:

—Expenditure increases should be limited on average to 2.5 percent a year through 1996.

—The tax moratorium will last until the end of the current legislative term; thereafter new financial benefits and improvements in existing benefits may only be enacted if balanced by similar cutbacks elsewhere.

—Subsidies to the Federal Employment Office are to be terminated through administrative and legal measures.

—The net deficit will be fixed at a maximum of DM 40 billion for 1993, and at an estimated DM 30 billion for 1994 and DM 25 billion for 1995.

June 3   The federal government decides to extend the 1992 Partnership for Eastern Renewal.

June 30   The 7.5 percent surcharge on personal and corporate income taxes, in effect since July 1, 1991, expires.

July 1   The Bundestag decides to increase basic housing rents in eastern Germany. Rents will rise on January 1, 1993, by at least DM 1.20 per square meter, and at the beginning of 1994 by another DM 0.60. At the beginning of 1995 all housing rents will be free.

October 22   The federal government and the new Länder agree to share the cost of environmental damages between these Länder (40 percent) and the Treuhandanstalt (60 percent).

November 27   The Bundestag passes the 1993 federal budget. Expenditures are planned to increase by 2.5 percent, to DM 435.6 billion. The net deficit will be DM 43 billion; because of cyclical effects this is DM 5 billion higher than originally planned. The government's contribution to the unemployment insurance system is lowered by DM 2.5 billion. This leads to a 0.2 percent increase in the contribution rate, which is balanced by a reduction in pension insurance contributions of the same magnitude.

December 2   The Bundestag passes an extension of (to 1996) and an increase in subsidies under the law on investment allowances for eastern Germany from an average of about 5 percent to 8 percent, and in certain cases up to 20 percent.

1993

March 4   The federal government introduces in the Bundestag a draft Law on the Reorganization of the Federal Consolidation Program (Gesetz zur Umsetzung des Föderalen Konsolidierungsprogramms, or FKPG), aimed at managing the financial burdens related to German unification, securing reconstruction in the new Länder, reorganizing the federal financial equalization scheme, and easing the burden on public budgets by enacting the following measures:

—To secure the long-term financing of eastern Germany's adjustment process, the German Unity Fund for 1993 and 1994 would be enlarged, and as of 1995 the new

Länder would become part of the federal financial equalization scheme.

—To manage the financial burden of the former East Germany, a Debt Redemption Fund (Erblastentilgungsfond) would assume the liabilities accumulated until December 31, 1994 in the Credit Liquidation Fund (Kreditabwicklungsfond) and the Treuhandanstalt. The federal government is responsible for the management of the fund, including the settlement of the debt.

—To consolidate the public budgets the following measures are planned: first, expenditure cuts of DM 4.2 billion in 1993, DM 5.7 billion in 1994, DM 6.8 billion in 1995, and DM 7 billion in 1996; second, a reduction of tax exemptions (generating additional revenues of DM 1.1 billion in 1994, DM 2.1 billion in 1995, and DM 2.2 billion in 1996); and third, a tax increase, in particular the introduction of a solidarity surcharge (*Solidaritätszuschlag*) of 4 percent on personal and corporate income taxes (additional revenues of DM 0.7 billion in 1993, DM 1.7 billion in 1994, DM 16.7 billion in 1995, and DM 18.1 billion in 1996).

March 11 The federal minister of the environment signs an administrative agreement that secures financing for environmental cleanup (*Altlastensanierung*) program in the new Länder. In the agreement, the federal government and the new Länder agree to provide DM 15 billion between 1993 and 1997 for this purpose.

March 13 The federal and state governments agree on a federal consolidation program. Its most important provisions are as follows:

—The German Unity Fund will be increased by DM 3.7 billion in 1993. For 1994 a further increase is planned: the federal government is prepared to transfer an additional DM 5.3 billion to eastern Germany, and the western German Länder have agreed to examine whether they could provide additional financial assistance beyond the DM 3.5 billion already guaranteed.

—After the expiration of the German Unity Fund, the new Länder would participate in the federal-state financial equalization scheme; it would be restructured in such a way that the new Länder would receive DM 55.8 billion in 1995. The Länder's share of VAT revenues would increase from 37 percent to 44 percent, at the expense of the federal government.

—Funding for the interest reduction program (Zinsverbilligungsprogramm) of the Kreditanstalt für Wiederaufbau (KfW), designed to support and modernize eastern German dwellings, and financed by the federal government, will be doubled from DM 30 billion to DM 60 billion. As of mid-1995 the federal government will assume DM 31 billion of the DM 51 billion debt of communal and cooperative housing companies of the former East Germany. Until then, the federal government and the new Länder will share the servicing of the outstanding credits.

—The Law Concerning Special Depreciation Allowances and Tax Deduction in the Assisted Area (Fördergebietsgesetz für Wohnungsbau- Investitionen im Privatvermögen), which provides for 50 percent of special exemptions within the first five years, will be extended for two years, to 1996.

—To sustain its labor market policy measures, the federal government provides an additional DM 2 billion in 1993 for the new Länder.

—To safeguard core industries and to provide for environmental cleanup in the former East Germany, the credit line of the Treuhandanstalt will be increased from DM 30 billion to DM 38 billion.

—At the center of the fiscal consolidation program is the introduction of a solidarity surcharge of 7.5 percent on personal and corporate income taxes beginning in January 1995 (to provide additional revenues of DM 28 billion). The wealth tax on private real and financial property would also be increased, while the level of tax exemption would be adjusted upward accordingly.

—To reach a consolidation volume of DM 9 billion, expenditures would be cut and tax privileges reduced; among other things this includes adjusting the insurance tax to the level of the VAT. Standard social benefits would not be affected by the cuts, but their misuse as well as the misappropriation of subsidies would be checked.

March 26 The Bundesrat passes the Law on Deregulation of Investments and Zoning (Gesetz zur Erleichterung von Investitionen und der Ausweisung und Bereitstellung von Wohnbauland). In effect beginning May 1, the law relaxes various restrictions on investments in housing development in the new Länder.

May 27 The Bundestag passes the federal consolidation act, the supplementary budget for fiscal year 1993, and the so-called German Competitiveness Act (*Standortsicherungsgesetz*); as its formal name ("Gesetz zur Verbesserung der steuerlichen Bediengungen zur Sicherung des Wirtschaftsstandorts Deutschland im Europäischen Binnenmarkt") suggests, the law is aimed at reforming the German tax code in order to improve the country's competitiveness within the European market.

—The FKPG regulates the financing of the eastern German adjustment process, the management of the financial burdens of the former East Germany, and the consolidation of the public sector budgets. It encompasses the following crucial measures:

—Beginning in 1995, the five new Länder will participate in the financial equalization scheme along with the federal government and the western German Länder. During the transition period the German Unity Fund will be increased again, by DM 3.7 billion for 1993 and DM 10.7 billion for 1994.

—In keeping with the federal-state agreements of March 13, the financial burden on housing construction companies is eased. Funding of the KfW program for the promotion and modernization of eastern German dwellings is increased to DM 60 billion, and an additional DM 2 billion is provided for labor market policies.

—Over a period of 15 years the federal government grants additional financial aid of DM 6.6 billion annually to the new Länder to compensate for differences in economic strength and to promote economic growth.

—The financial burdens resulting from the Treuhandanstalt and the Credit Liquidation Fund will be covered by the Debt Redemption Fund.

—The FKPG will generate savings of DM 1 billion in 1993, DM 2.8 billion in 1994, and DM 3.4 billion in 1995. These will come from, among other things, cuts in welfare benefits and in subsidies to agriculture and mining, and expenditure reductions caused by deferred income adjustments for civil servants and improved prevention of abuse of unemployment insurance benefits.

The law calls for the following changes in taxation:

—the collection of a solidarity surcharge on personal and corporate income taxes of 7.5 percent beginning on January 1, 1995 (providing additional revenues for 1995 of DM 28 billion);

—an increase in the insurance tax rate (excluding fire insurance) by 2 percentage points, to 12 percent, beginning on July 1, 1993, and an additional 3 percentage points after January 1, 1995 (additional revenues of DM 650 million in 1993, DM 1.65 billion in 1994, and DM 4.05 billion in 1995);

—a doubling of taxes on private wealth by 0.5 percentage point to 1 percent, accompanied by a rise in the level of exemptions (additional revenues of DM 1 billion in 1995);

—a reduction in the assessment basis used in tax-induced promotion to purchase old buildings from DM 330,000 to DM 150,000, beginning in 1994 (additional revenues of DM 160 million in 1994, DM 350 million in 1995, and DM 550,000 in 1996);

—persons with incomes below the poverty level are exempted from income taxes as a consequence of the ruling by the constitutional court on September 25, 1992 (causing a reduction in revenues of DM 2.2 billion in 1993, DM 3.1 billion in 1994, and DM 3.8 billion in 1995).

The supplementary budget for fiscal year 1993 provides that:

—The budget volume of DM 458.1 billion and the net deficit of DM 67.8 billion, which exceed previously budgeted amounts, are augmented by DM 22.5 billion and DM 24.6 billion, respectively; the principal reason for the shortfall is reconstruction assistance to the new Länder (among other things, the local investment subsidy of DM 1.5 billion) and cyclically induced increases in expenditures as well as losses in revenues.

Provisions of the German Competitiveness Act include the reform of corporate taxation in revenue-neutral fashion; the tax reform includes the following crucial measures, envisioned to take effect on January 1, 1994:

—a reduction in the corporate income tax rate for withheld profits from 50 percent to 44 percent, and in that for distributed profits from 36 percent to 30 percent;

—a reduction in the top rate of the trade tax from 53 percent to 44 percent, and the introduction of a depreciation allowance on savings for small and middle-sized businesses to reinvest in new equipment;

—introduction of an exemption for corporate operating assets of DM 500,000 per business, and a 25 percent deduction when assessing the operating assets for inheritance tax purposes;

—a waiver on the collection of trade capital taxes and wealth taxes in the new Länder until the end of 1995, as well as extension of the special depreciation allowances for economic goods of corporate assets until the end of 1996;

—a reduction of the digressive depreciation for corporate buildings from 10 percent to 7 percent in the initial years as well as a limitation on the digressive depreciation for mobile economic goods of the fixed assets from a maximum of 30 percent— three times what would be allowed under a linear depreciation—to a maximum of 25 percent to counterfinance measures taken to ease the tax burden.

June 23 The federal government decides to increase the mineral oil tax on gasoline by 16 pfennigs per liter and that on diesel by 7 pfennigs per liter, as well as to raise the motor vehicle tax for diesel automobiles by DM 7.50 per 100 cubic centimeters of engine displacement starting January 1, 1994. The additional revenues of DM 8.5 billion are intended to defray the old debts of the Bundesbahn (the federal railways).

June 29 The federal government decides on a savings, consolidation, and growth program (Spar-, Konsolidierungs-, und Wachstumsprogram, or SKWP) to limit new federal indebtedness in 1994 to DM 67.5 billion (equivalent to the 1993 level). The budgetary savings for the federal government will amount to DM 21 billion in 1994, DM 27.4 billion in 1995, and DM 28.8 billion in 1996; for all territorial authorities the savings will amount to DM 25.3 billion in 1994, DM 32.7 billion in 1995, and DM 34.6 billion in 1996.

The emphasis of the consolidation is on social benefits. The following measures are planned, among others:

—a reduction in wage substitution benefits, benefits for short-time workers, integration benefits and support, bad weather benefits, and unemployment benefits by 3 percentage points as well as a digressive structuring of unemployment benefits (savings of DM 1.47 billion expected in 1994, and DM 1.3 billion in 1995);

—unemployment benefits will be granted for a maximum of two years (savings of DM 1.3 billion in 1994, and DM 1.3 billion in 1995);

—a reduction of expenditures for employment creation programs;

—elimination of "original" unemployment benefits (e.g., to civil servants reentering the private sector and to noncareer military personnel (savings of DM 1.7 billion in 1994 and DM 2.5 billion in 1995);

—reversal of the decrease in the unemployment insurance contribution rate from 6.5 percent to 6.3 percent, originally planned for January 1, 1994 (additional revenues of DM 2.5 billion in 1994, and DM 2.6 billion in 1995);

—stronger consideration of children's earnings when calculating child benefits (savings of DM 1 billion in 1994, and DM 1 billion in 1995).

Total budgetary relief resulting from cuts in social benefits and the reversal of the decrease in the unemployment insurance contribution rate is expected to amount to DM 22.5 billion in 1994, DM 27.4 billion in 1995, and DM 26.1 billion in 1996. Additional savings are to be achieved through the limitation of government consumption, especially through a "zero round" of civil servants' incomes (savings of DM 3.2 billion in 1994), reductions of subsidies and similar special benefits (savings of DM 1.3 billion in 1994, DM 2.1 billion in 1995, and DM 2.9 billion in 1996), as well as numerous tax measures (additional revenues of DM 2.8 billion in 1994, DM 5.2 billion in 1995, and DM 5.8 billion in 1996).

June 30 The conference committee of the upper and lower houses of the legislature submits a compromise proposal for the German Competitiveness Act, with the following changes from the law that the Bundestag passed on May 27:

—The top corporate income tax rate is lowered from 53 percent to 47 percent, instead of to 44 percent. The rate of retained profits regarding the corporate income tax is decreased from 50 percent to 45 percent instead of to 44 percent. The corporate tax rate that is not subject to indirect relief is dropped from 46 percent to 42 percent instead of to 41 percent.

—The savings depreciation for small and middle-sized businesses to invest in new equipment will be introduced on January 1, 1995, one year later than originally planned.

—The digressive depreciation for mobile economic goods is reduced from 30 percent to 25 percent, which was designed to partially ease the tax burden.

—In the short term, public sector budgets will be burdened by the measures (revenue losses of DM 3.8 billion are projected in 1994, DM 5.6 billion in 1995, and DM 5.0 billion in 1996). In the medium term a small surplus is expected.

July 13 The federal government submits a draft of the federal budget for fiscal year 1994 and of the financial plan until 1997. In the 1994 federal budget, expenditures are fixed at DM 478.4 billion. This amounts to an increase of 4.4 percent from 1993 (2.6 percent if the reform of the federal railways is excluded). Net borrowing is planned at DM 67.5 billion, equal to 1993.

In the financial plan, the increase in expenditures between 1995 and 1997 is limited to an annual average of 1.5 percent; net borrowing is reduced gradually to DM 38 billion by 1997.

September 3 The federal government submits two bills to implement the SKWP of June 29. The first bill (1.SKWPG) contains those amendments that do not need to be confirmed by the Bundesrat. For the most part these are cuts in the budget of the Federal Employment Agency, child benefits, and education allowances. In addition, the 1.SKWPG contains the fuel tax increase linked to the railways reform. The second bill (2.SKWPG) encompasses those amendments that do need to be ratified by the Bundesrat, including the cuts in social benefits and maternity allowances.

September 27 The federal government submits the Draft Law on the Control of Tax Abuse and on Reform of the Tax Code (Entwurf eines Gesetzes zur Bekämpfung des Mißbrauchs und zur Bereinigung des Steuerrechts, or StMBG). The proposal would provide budget relief of DM 300 million in 1994, DM 1.1 billion in 1995, DM 1.7 billion in 1996, and DM 2.1 billion in 1997.

November 26 The Bundestag passes the federal budget for fiscal year 1994, in which federal expenditures increase by 4.8 percent, to DM 480 billion. The spending plan is based on the bills to implement the SKWP. In addition, a general but unspecified expenditure cut of DM 5 billion is erased. Net borrowing amounts to DM 69.1 billion. The Bundesrat rejects the 2.SKWPG and the StMBG because they would shift expenditures from the federal government and the Federal Employment Agency to local communities. It also expresses disapproval of the 1.SKWPG.

December 17 The Bundesrat agrees to a compromise submitted by the conference committee regarding the 1.SKWPG, the 2.SKWPG, the StMBG, and the fiscal 1994 federal budget.

The budgetary relief in 1994 from the SKWP is expected to amount to DM 20.9 billion for the federal government and DM 25.7 billion for all territorial authorities. Savings are expected to increase to DM 24.8 billion for the federal government and to DM 34.1 billion for all territorial units. As a result of the compromise negotiated in committee, the savings generated by the SKWP are DM 2.7 billion lower in fiscal 1994 than anticipated. The compromise contains the following changes:

—Unemployment benefits will not be restricted to two years and instead will remain unlimited in duration.

—"Original" unemployment benefits will not be canceled but instead will be limited to a maximum of one year.

—The intended "zero rounds" for social welfare rates are dropped. The rates are planned to be raised in mid-1994 and mid-1995 by 2 percent each year. The maximum increase is not to exceed the increase in net wages.

—The budgetary relief provided by the StMBG is expected to amount to DM 1.6 billion in 1994, DM 2.8 billion in 1995, DM 3.3 billion in 1996, and DM 3.7 billion in 1997.

The relief provided by the StMBG consists of:

—measures to consolidate the budget, to control abuse of and simplify the tax system, and to adjust and streamline tax laws (raising additional revenues of DM 2.1 billion in 1994, rising to DM 5.3 billion in 1997);

—a reduction in the motor vehicle tax for trucks and increases in the motor vehicle tax for diesel automobiles and in the kilometer flat charge for commuters from home to the workplace (reducing revenues by DM 500 million in 1994, to DM 1.6 billion in 1997).

The federal budget for fiscal 1994 lacks coverage for a total of DM 7.5 billion in expenditures. Coverage will be provided by savings in the execution of the budget in order to limit net borrowing to DM 69.1 billion.

The Bundesrat agrees to the railroad reform. The special funds *(Sondervermögen)* for the Deutsche Bundesbahn and the Deutsche Reichsbahn are merged into the Deutsche Bahn AG (German Railways, Inc.). For the time being, the additional expenses caused by railroad reform are covered by the fuel tax increase.

1994

January 1   The German Competitiveness Act, the 1.SKWPG, the 2.SKWPG, and the StMBG and the railway reform enter into force. The pension insurance contribution rate is increased from 17.5 percent to 19.2 percent.

Notes

Introduction

1. The protocol of the Maastricht Treaty on excessive deficit procedures states—with some qualifications—that the deficit-GDP ratio may not exceed 3 percent. In addition, the gross indebtedness of a country should not surpass 60 percent by the end of 1999. None of the member countries with the exception of Luxembourg had fulfilled both of these requirements at the end of 1993; see "The Second Stage of European Economic and Monetary Union," *Deutsche Bundesbank Monthly Report*, vol. 46 (January 1994), p. 27 (table).

Chapter I

1. See, for example, E. Pond, *Beyond the Wall: Germany's Road to Unification* (Brookings, 1993), pp. 225ff.

2 See, for example, K. Löbbe and others, Strukturwandel in *der Krise, Untersuchungen des Rheinisch-Westfälischen Instituts für Wirtschaftsforschung 9* (Essen: RWI, 1993), pp. 259ff. See also Deutsches Institut für Wirtschaftsforschung, Institut für Weltwirtschaft at the University of Kiel in cooperation with the Institut für Wirtschaftsforschung Halle, "Gesamtwirtschaftliche und unternehmerische Anpassungsfortschritte in Ostdeutschland—Neunter Bericht," *DIW-Wochenbericht*, vol. 60 (1993), pp. 554ff.

3. Such a comparison, however, fails to take into account the differences in the work week and work year between east and west: on average, the work week in the east exceeded that in the west by two hours in 1993; and annual leave in the east was about one week less than in the west. See H. Kohler, "Jahresarbeitszeit und Arbeitsvolumen sowie ihre Komponenten. Eine empirische Analyse der aktuellen Entwicklung mit einer Vorausschau auf 1993," *IAB-Werkstattbericht*, 17 (Nuremberg: IAB, 1993), p. 3.

4. See W.H. Reinicke, *Building a New Europe: The Challenge of System Transformation and Systemic Reform* (Brookings, 1992), and "Western Reluctance to Economic Integration: A Possible Way Out," paper presented to a CeSPI Conference on "Assessing European Security Five Years After 1989: Current Failures and the Need for a New Strategy vis-à-vis the East," Rome, June 24-25, 1994.

5. These figures are based on the authors' calculations drawn from *Die Lage der Weltwirtschaft und der deutschen Wirtschaft im Herbst 1993* (Essen, 1993). This analysis of the economic situation was conducted by the following members of the Arbeitsgemeinschaft deutscher wirtschaftswissenschaftlicher Forschungsinstitute e.V.,

Munich: Deutsches Institut für Wirtschaftsforschung, Berlin (Institut für Konjunkturforschung); HWWA-Institut für Wirtschaftsforschung, Hamburg; ifo Institut für Wirtschaftsforschung, Munich; Institut für Weltwirtschaft at the University of Kiel; Institut für Wirtschaftsforschung, Halle; Rheinisch-Westfälisches Institut für Wirtschaftsforschung, Essen. The calculations do not include the payments for the withdrawal of former Soviet troops from the Federal Republic between 1991 and 1994, which amounted to DM 15 billion; see Bundesministerium der Finanzen, *Finanzbericht 1991* (Bonn, 1990), p. 15. Additional revenues of about DM 50 billion per year in taxes, social security insurance, etc., which are a direct result of the expenditures in the east would have to be balanced against the transfer payments; see U. Heilemann and R. Jochimsen, *Christmas in July? The Political Economy of German Unification Reconsidered*, Brookings Occasional Papers (1993), p. 24, table 4.

6. See Bundesministerium der Finanzen, *Finanzbericht 1994* (Bonn, 1993), p. 11.

7. See, for example, Wissenschaftlicher Beirat beim Bundesministerium der Wirtschaft, *Gesamtwirtschaftliche Orientierung bei drohender finanzieller Überforderung*, Studienreihe des Bundesministeriums der Wirtschaft 178 (Bonn: Stollfuß, 1992); Wissenschaftlicher Beirat beim Bundesministerium der Finanzen, *Perspektiven staatlicher Ausgabepolitik*, Schriftenreihe des Bundesministeriums der Finanzen 51 (Bonn: Stollfuß, 1992); and K. F. Viermetz, "Die Vereinigung hat Deutschland geschwächt," Die Bank (1993), pp. 69ff.

8. However, David Roche of Morgan Stanley provided a remarkably accurate estimate of the costs of unification in 1990. He calculated the "current social expenses" and the "costs of reconstruction" in the former East Germany to amount to between 5 and 6 percent of GNP. See Klaus von Dohnanyi, *Das deutsche Wagnis* (Munich: Knaur, 1991), pp. 270ff.

9. See the appendix. It is noteworthy that a substantial number of financing decisions were made within the framework of the federal budget legislation. Special policy decisions like the creation of the German Unity Fund or the Federal Consolidation Program (Föderale Konsolidierungsprogramm, or FKP), were the exception.

10. A more detailed examination of these reasons lies beyond the scope of this study. See, for example, W. Hankel, *Die Sieben Todsünden der Vereinigung* (Berlin: Siedler, 1993), and Heilemann and Jochimsen, *Christmas in July?* p. 9, and the literature cited there.

11. See, for example, B. Fritzsche and others, "Perspektiven und Optionen der deutschen Finanzpolitik," *Wirtschaftsdienst*, vol. 71 (1991), pp. 20ff.

12. See Heilemann and Jochimsen, *Christmas in July?* p. 24, table 4.

13. See Bundesministerium der Finanzen, *Finanzbericht 1991*, pp. 12ff.

14. The immediate effects on inflation of the financial transfer from the west to the east were small despite the strained capacity utilization in western Germany; see Fritzsche and others, "Perspektiven," p. 27. This is not the case, however, with the indirect effects, a consequence of numerous tax increases and their at least partly successful rollover into wages (see below).

15. See G. Barabas, U. Heilemann, and H. D. v. Loeffelholz, "Optimal Finance and German Unification," paper presented at the International Symposium on Economic Modelling, University of Piraeus, Athens, June 2-4, 1993.

16. For the historical experience see the comments by Adam Smith on the financing of a sudden economic shock, in this case the outbreak of war: "An immediate and great expence must be incurred in that moment of immediate danger, which will not wait for the gradual and slow returns of the new taxes. In this exigency government can have no other resources but in borrowing. . . . The ordinary expence of the greater part of modern governments in time of peace being equal or nearly equal to their ordinary revenue, when war comes, they are both unwilling and unable to increase their revenue in proportion to the increase of their expence. They are unwilling for fear of offending the people by so great and so sudden an increase of taxes, would soon be disgusted with the war; and they are unable, from not well knowing what taxes would be sufficient to produce the revenue wanted. The facility of borrowing delivers them from the embarrassment which this fear and inability would otherwise occasion. By means of borrowing they are enabled, with a very moderate increase in taxes, to raise from year to year, money sufficient for carrying on the war, and by the practice of perpetual funding they are enabled, with the smallest possible increase in taxes, to raise annually the largest possible sum of money . . . ." Adam Smith, *The Wealth of Nations*, 6th ed., vol. 2 (London: Methuen, 1961; E. Cannan, ed.), pp. 444ff. On the actual evidence, see for example H. Teltschik, *329 Tage: Innenansichten der Einigung* (Munich: Goldmann, 1993), p. 270, and W. Schäuble, *Der Vertrag: Wie ich über die deutsche Einheit verhandelte* (Stuttgart: Deutsche Verlagsanstalt, 1991), pp. 184ff.

17. See the references in Heilemann and Jochimsen, *Christmas in July?* pp. 20ff.

18. Evaluations of the interest rate effects of unification range from an increase in the long-term German real interest rate by 1.7 percent to no effects at all. For the underlying assumptions about impulses, the effects of exchange rates, and the models used to estimate the effects on interest rates caused by unification, see U. Heilemann, "The Economics of German Unification," *Konjunkturpolitik*, vol. 37 (1991), pp. 138ff; Heilemann and Jochimsen, *Christmas in July?* pp. 26ff; J.-P. Fitoussi and others, *Competitive Disinflation: The Mark and the Budgetary Politics in Europe*, International Policy Group of OFCE (Oxford University Press, 1993), p. 50; and J. Kröger, "Integration Problems of the East and West German Economy," *Rivista di Politica Economica*, May 1991, pp. 198ff.

19. See, for example, G. A. Horn, W. Scheremet, and R. Zwiener, *Domestic and International Effects of German Monetary and Social Union*, DIW Discussion Paper 26 (Berlin, 1991); W. J. McKibbin, *The New Europe and Its Economic Implications for the World Economy*, (Brookings and Congressional Budget Office, June 1991); and Deutsche Bundesbank, "Der Einfluss des deutschen Vereinigungsprozesses auf die wirtschaftliche Entwicklung in den europäischen Partnerländern," *Monatsbericht*, vol. 44 (July 1992), pp. 23ff.

20. See Fritzsche and others, "Perspektiven," pp. 26ff.

21. See, for example, H. Gebhardt, U. Heilemann, and H. D. v. Loeffelholz, "Finanzhilfe der Bundesrepublik für die DDR: Umfang, Formen, Wirkungen," *RWI-Mitteilungen*, vol. 40 (1989), p. 348, and Sachverständigenrat zur Begutachtung der gesamtwirtschaftlichen Entwicklung, "Jahresgutachten 1990/91," *BT-Drucksache* 11, 8472 (Bonn, 1990), Ziffer 34ff.

22. Based on the financial planning of the summer of 1993, simulations with the RWI

business cycle model led to the conclusion that the macroeconomic developments in 1993 were little affected by the planned policy measures (among others, the FKP and the SKWP [the saving, consolidation, and growth program]). The calculations showed, however, that real GNP growth would be slowed by 1.5 percentage points and 3 percentage points in 1994 and 1995, respectively. Of course, any relaxation of monetary policy in response to the consolidation measures would have tended to offset this reduction in growth; see Rheinisch-Westfälisches Institut für Wirtschaftsforschung, *Konjunkturberichte*, vol. 44 (1993), pp. 41ff.

23. For the overall economic potential of current infrastructure capacity see, for example, K. Löbbe and others, *Strukturwandel in der Krise*, pp. 253ff.

24. For more details see, for example, the table in Rheinisch-Westfälisches Institut für Wirtschaftsforschung, Konjunkturberichte, 44 (1993), p. 184.

25. See, for example, Sachverständigenrat zur Begutachtung der gesamtwirtschaftlichen Entwicklung, "Jahresgutachten 1992/93," BT-Drucksache 12/3774 (Bonn, 1992), Ziffer 208ff; see also B. Fritzsche, "Wer finanziert die deutsche Einheit? Zur Diskussion um die 'Gerechtigkeitslücke'" *RWI-Konjunkturbrief*, no. 2 (1992).

26. See, for example, *Economic Report of the President, February 1994* (Government Printing Office, 1994), pp. 81ff.

27. For example, a study by the Federal Reserve Board of New York finds that the U.S. budget deficits in the 1980s reduced real net income in 1990 only by 3 percent. See P. Krugman, *Peddling Prosperity: Economic Sense and Nonsense in the Age of Diminished Expectations* (Norton, 1994), p. 128.

28. See, for example, B. Bosworth, *Saving and Investment in a Global Economy* (Brookings, 1993), pp. 53ff, and M. Goldstein and M. Mussa, "The Integration of World Capital Markets," *IMF Working Paper WP/93/95* (Washington, 1993) and the literature cited therein.

29. See, for example, R. Solomon, "Do We Face a Global Shortage of Capital?" Brookings Discussion Papers in International Economics 91 (1991). On the basis of estimates by the Organization for Economic Cooperation and Development and the International Monetary Fund, Solomon expects a worldwide increase of current account deficits, or national savings deficits, from about $80 billion in 1989-90 to between $150 billion and $216 billion in 1994. He estimates the savings gap for the Federal Republic at between $60 billion and $70 billion. However, the analysis does not address to what extent these deficits would be reduced if the current slump in the world economy is overcome, nor does it consider the rate effects of these deficits, considering total world savings of about $4.5 trillion (1989).

30. For an earlier discussion of the financing of German unification see, for example, J. Priewe and R. Hickel, *Der Preis der Einheit* (Frankfurt am Main: Fischer-Taschenbuch, 1991), pp. 133ff.

31. R. Dornbusch, "The End of the German Miracle," *Journal of Economic Literature*, vol. 31 (1993), p. 881.

32. See for example, Sachverständigenrat zur Begutachtung der Gesamtwirtschaftlichen Entwicklung, *Jahresgutachten 1992/93*, Ziffer 363ff.

Chapter II

1. Consider here, for example, the connection between earned income and taxation. See, among others, W. Franz, *Arbeitsmarktökonomik* (Berlin: Springer, 1991), pp. 48ff.

2. On the introduction of direct taxes in Germany see F. Neumark, "Die Finanzpolitik in der Zeit vor dem ersten Weltkrieg," in Deutsche Bundesbank, *Währung und Wirtschaft in Deutschland* (Frankfurt am Main: Knapp, 1976), pp. 83ff. For a skeptical account of tax policy in the Reagan era with respect to the linkage between taxes and economic behavior and the income effects of tax reductions, see *Economic Report of the President, 1994*, pp. 87ff.

3. Compare here also the discussion of supply-side effects in macroeconometric models. See, for example, O. Eckstein, *The DRI Model of the U.S. Economy* (New York: McGraw-Hill, 1983), pp. 56ff.

4. See B. Fritzsche and others, "Perspektiven und Optionen der deutschen Finanzpolitik 1991 bis 1994," *Wirtschaftsdienst*, vol. 71 (1991), pp. 26ff.

5. See, for example, Rheinisch-Westfälisches Institut für Wirtschaftsforschung, *Konjunkturberichte*, vol. 44 (1993), pp.14ff, and Bundesregierung, *Jahreswirtschaftsbericht 1994*, BT-Drucksache 12/6676 (Bonn, 1994), pp. 46ff.

6. See here, for example, Bundesministerium für Wirtschaft, *Strategie für den Standort Deutschland: Wirtschaftspolitik für die neunziger Jahre* (Bonn, 1992) and *Zukunftssicherung des Standortes Deutschland* (Bonn, 1993); and Bibliothek des Instituts für Weltwirtschaft an der Universität Kiel, "Standort D.: Bibliographie zur Internationalen Wettbewerbsfähigkeit der deutschen Wirtschaft," Kieler Bibliographien zu aktuellen ökonomischen Themen 12 (Kiel, 1993).

7. See, for example, S. Kuznets, "Concepts and Assumptions in Long-Term Projections of National Product," in *Long-Range Economic Projection*, Studies in Income and Wealth 16 (Columbia University, 1954), pp. 9ff. Medium- and long-term econometric models usually do not make such assumptions. However, because of the wage-employment connection they inherently tend—in the (very) long run—toward equilibrium (full employment).

8. See, for example, E. M. Verkade, "Restructuring the East German Economy— Some Model Results," Research Memorandum 80 (The Hague, 1991); R. Barro and X. Sala-I-Martin, "Convergence across States and Regions," *Brookings Papers on Economic Activity* (1992), pp. 107ff; and R. Dornbusch and H. Wolff, "Economic Transition in Eastern Germany," *Brookings Papers on Economic Activity* (1992), pp. 235ff.

9. See Commission of the European Communities, *Growth, Competitiveness, Employment: The Challenges and Ways Forward into the 21st Century*, White Paper, COM(93) 700 final (Brussels, 5 December 1993), pp. 9ff.

10. See the reference to the works of Niskanen, Tollison, Wagner and others, Alesina and Tabellini, Saunders and Klau, Alesina and Drazen, and Corsetti and Roubini, among others, in J. de Haan, C. G. M. Sterks, and C. A. de Kam, "Towards Budget Discipline: An Economic Assessment of the Possibilities for Reducing National Deficits in the Run-Up to EMU," *Economic Papers 99* (Brussels, 1992), pp. 36ff.

11. Bundesministerium der Finanzen, *Finanzbericht 1994* (Bonn, 1994), pp. 69ff.

12. For the range of growth prognoses under current discussion for the Federal Republic and for western Germany alone see U. Heilemann, "Mo' Money? Medium Term Perspectives of the West German Economy," *Economie Appliquée*, vol. 46 (1993), no. 1, pp. 63ff. A similar conclusion is reached in Prognos AG, *Industrial Countries* (Basel: Prognos, 1991) and in the forecast of the Federal Employment Agency in D. Bogai and others, "Arbeitsplatzförderung statt Lohnersatz," IAB-Werkstatt-Bericht 7 (1992).

13. Since 1960, the annual average expansion rate of real GDP during the upswing amounted to 4 percent.

14. Deliveries from the west to the east are considered exports according to the system of national accounts.

15. This assumption has already been falsified by current developments (see below).

16. See B. Hillebrand and others, *Strukturpolitische Restriktionen für ökonomische Instrumente zur CO_2-Minderung. 1. Zwischenbericht zum Forschungsvorhaben Nr. 101 03 163 des UFOPLAN des Umweltbundesamtes* (Essen: RWI, 1993), pp. 77ff.

17. See B. Hillebrand, M. Kiy, und R. Neuhaus, "Das RWI-Strukturmodel," RWI-Papiere 19 (Essen: RWI, 1988).

18. There are few reliable data for medium-term forecasts. In the case of one- and two-year forecasts, the margin of error in the estimated change in GNP/GDP growth rates is about 1 percent.

19. See Bundesministerium der Finanzen, *Finanzbericht 1994*, pp. 69ff. Other forecasts containing the necessary details are not available.

20. Bundesministerium der Finanzen, *Finanzbericht 1994*, p. 11.

21. See Heilemann and Jochimsen, *Christmas in July?* p. 24, table 4.

22. See Bundesministerium der Finanzen, *Ausgaben des Bundes für die jungen Länder 1992 bis 1994. Stand: 9. Juli 1993* (mimeo).

23. For the development of the debt positions of the Treuhandanstalt and the other supplementary budgets until the end of 1992, see Deutsche Bundesbank, "The Significance of Subsidiary Budgets in the Context of German Unification," *Monatsbericht*, vol. 45 (May 1993), pp. 43ff.

24. See Deutsche Bundesbank, "The Economic Scene in Germany in Winter 1993-4," *Deutsche Bundesbank Monthly Report*, vol. 46 (February 1994), p. 42.

25. The difference in the size of the deficit reported in the financial statistics and in the national income accounts is due to the fact that credits and income from investments are considered expenditures in the former, but savings in the latter. Another difference is that amounts are recorded at the time of payment in the financial statistics, and at the time of origin in national income accounting. For more details see H. Essig, "Finanzierungssalden für den öffentlichen Bereich in den Volkswirtschaftlichen Gesamtrechnungen und in der Finanzstatistik," *Wirtschaft und Statistik* (1990), pp. 383ff.

26. Sachverständigenrat zur Begutachtung der gesamtwirtschaftlichen Entwicklung, *Weiter auf Wachstumskurs—Jahresgutachten 1986/87* (Stuttgart: Kohlhammer, 1986), no. 278.

27. See Bundesministerium der Finanzen, *Finanzbericht 1994*, pp. 11ff.

28. See Gemeinschaftsdiagnose, *Frühjahr 1993*, p. 26 (table). The analysis is based on a (nominal) GDP growth of 5 percent—similar to the growth rate assumed in this study.

29. For example, critics have argued that greater consideration should be given to the

solvency or economic quality of public sector assets; see, for example, W. Buiter, "A Guide to Public Sector Debts and Deficits," *Economic Policy*, vol. 1 (1985), pp. 13ff; and L. Kotlikoff, "The Economic Impact of Deficit Finance," *IMF Working Paper DM/84/24* (Washington, April 1984).

30. The monetary reform did not convert into deutsche marks the very large debts of the Third Reich that had accumulated in the course of rearmament and during World War II. The reichsmark debts of the states and local communities were comparably low at the time. Their conversion at a rate of 10 to 1 reduced them to a negligible amount; see W. Dreissig, "Zur Entwicklung der öffentlichen Finanzwirtschaft seit dem Jahre 1950," in Deutsche Bundesbank, *Währung und Wirtschaft in Deutschland 1876-1975*, p. 728.

31. In August 1952 a capital levy was implemented in order to compensate for war damages. The overall payments amounted to about DM 130 billion. For this and other compensatory measures see W. Dreissig, "Zur Entwicklung der öffentlichen Finanzwirtschaft," p. 714, and W. Albers, "Der Lastenausgleich: Rückblick und Beurteilung," *Finanzarchiv*, Bd. 47, N.F. (1991), pp. 272ff.

32. See C. Kindleberger, *A Financial History of Western Europe*, 2nd ed. (Oxford University Press, 1993), pp. 404ff.

33. See F. Neumark, *Die Finanzpolitik in der Zeit vor dem ersten Weltkrieg*, p. 100.

34. An adjustment of the deficits, for example, for the effects of underemployment is not considered here. In the case of the United States a budget deficit of 4 percent of GNP in fiscal 1993 is projected to decline to about 2.3 percent by the late 1990s; see *Economic Report of the President, 1994*, pp. 75ff.

35. See the data provided by the Organization for Economic Cooperation and Development, cited in W. Buiter, "Public Debt in the US. How Much, How Bad and Who Pays?" NBER Working Paper 4362 (Cambridge: National Bureau of Economic Research, 1993), table 2. For the deficit and debt situation of the EU countries, see also J. de Haan and others, *Towards Budget Discipline*, pp. 11ff. Statistics on federal debts and deficits are only partially comparable across countries for a number of reasons, most importantly because of differennces in the importance of social security budgets. In addition, important obligations such as pension and retirement liabilities of the public and private sectors generally are ignored entirely. See, for example, H. Bohn, "Budget Deficits and Government Accounting," *Carnegie-Rochester Conference Series on Public Policy*, vol. 37 (1992), pp. 1ff. Estimates by CS First Boston concluded that the debt-GNP ratio of the Federal Republic in 1990 was more than three times as high as reported (179 percent instead of 44 percent) if one took into account pension and retirement liabilities. The same holds true for other European countries; see CS First Boston Economic Research, *The Remaking of Europe—Employment and Hidden Debt* (London, 1993), p. 7. Similar results (indebtedness levels 3.3 times nominal GNP in 1988) can be found in H. W. Müller and U. Roppel, "Eine Abschätzung des Kapitalbedarfs bei einer vollständigen Kapitaldeckung der geleisteten Rentenversicherung," in B. Felderer (ed.), Bevölkerung und Wirtschaft, *Schriften des Vereins für Sozialpolitik*, N.F. 202 (Berlin: Dunker & Humblot, 1990), p. 438. It should also be noted that the public debts reported usually are gross debts. German net indebtedness in 1993 is estimated to have been less than 60 percent of the gross debt; see W. Horstmann and F. Schneider, *Deficits, Bailout and Free Riders: Fiscal Elements of a European Constitution* (Kyklos, 1994), vol. 47, p. 358.

Estimates that include, for example, short-term holdings of the public sector are, however, highly suspect.

36. See *Economic Report of the President, 1994*, p. 75.

37. See *Economic Report of the President, 1994*, pp. 360ff, and calculations by the authors.

38. See, for example, M. Boskin, *Reagan and the Economy—The Successes, Failures and Unfinished Agenda* (San Francisco: ICS Press, 1989), pp. 187ff; B. M. Friedman, *Day of Reckoning—The Consequences of American Economic Policy Under Reagan and After*, 2nd ed. (Vintage Books, 1989), pp. 79ff; and, especially on the twin deficits, P. Krugman, *The Age of Diminished Expectations: U.S. Economic Policy in the 1990s* (Cambridge: MIT Press, 1992), pp. 42ff; and, most recently, *Economic Report of the President, 1994*, pp. 26ff.

39. See especially Friedman, *Day of Reckoning*, pp. 209ff.

40. See Krugman, *The Age of Diminished Expectations*, p. 191.

41. See *Deutsche Bundesbank Monthly Report*, vol. 45 (November 1993), p. 73.

42. See, for example, "Revenue from and Economic Implications of Tax on Interest Income," *Deutsche Bundesbank Monthly Report*, vol. 46 (January 1993), pp. 50ff.

43. Note that the debtors are for the most part the territorial units of government. The social security budgets cannot incur debts.

44. In 1993 purchases of securities by foreigners in the Federal Republic reached a new high of DM 246 billion (compared with DM 127 billion in 1992); 93 percent of these were fixed-interest securities, mostly government bonds (DM 165 billion); see "Deutschland als Kapitalmagnet," *Neue Zürcher Zeitung*, Fernausgabe no. 72 (March 27/28, 1994).

45. For a general discussion of the issue see Wissenschaftlicher Beirat beim Bundesministerium der Finanzen, "Gutachten zur Schuldenstrukturpolitik des Staates," *Schriftenreihe des Bundesministeriums der Finanzen* 27 (Bonn: Stollfuß Verlag, 1979), pp. 42ff.

46. This may not apply to the Bundesbank, however, which is worried that its ability to implement interest rate increases at whatever time it deems appropriate is limited due to the rising short-term indebtedness of the federal government; see, for example, "Bundesbank gegen kurzfristige Staatsverschuldung," *Frankfurter Allgemeine Zeitung* (March 10, 1994).

47. See U. Heilemann and B. Hüttebräuker, "'Operation '82' und 'Beschäftigungsinitiative'—eine ökonometrische Analyse ihrer gesamtwirtschaftlichen Auswirkungen in den Jahren 1982 und 1983," *RWI-Mitteilungen*, vol. 32 (1981), pp. 221ff. For the primary effects see also H. Gebhardt, "Finanzpolitik nach dem Regierungswechsel," *RWI-Mitteilungen*, vol. 40 (1989), p. 47.

48. See Bundesministerium der Finanzen, *Finanzbericht 1994*, pp. 15ff.

49. Bundesministerium der Finanzen, *Finanzbericht 1994*, p. 15.

50. Bundesministerium der Finanzen, *Finanzbericht 1994*, p. 16.

51. Note that this does not include DM 15 billion for military procurement, maintenance of equipment, military research and development, and military bases until 1997; these expenditures are not considered investments in fiscal planning.

52. A similar detailed plan for state and local governments is not available at the present time.

53. See "The Financial Relations of the Federal Republic of Germany with the European Communities since 1988," *Deutsche Bundesbank Monthly Report*, vol. 45 (November 1993), pp. 61ff. The Bundesbank anticipates an increase in net contributions from DM 6.1 billion in 1992 to DM 22.2 billion in 1997 (p. 70).

54. See Bundesministerium der Finanzen, *Finanzbericht 1994*, p. 42.

55. On the critical situation in the western German communities with respect to investment possibilities and their revenue prospects (allotments by the Länder), see, for example, U. Heilemann, H. D. von Loeffelholz, und H. Rappen, "Finanzielle Auswirkungen des Föderalen Konsolidierungsprogramms auf die Gemeinden und die Gemeindeverbände—dargestellt am Beispiel Nordrhein-Westfalens," *Der Gemeindehaushalt*, vol. 94 (1993), pp. 193ff.

56. See B. Fritzsche, *Wer finanziert die deutsche Einheit?* pp. 2ff.

57. See Bundesministerium der Finanzen, *Finanzbericht 1990*, pp. 12ff.

58. In most cases the high rates of increase in such areas as pension insurance for workers and employees, agricultural social policy, promotion of small and medium-sized enterprises, regional aid, guarantees and other policies to promote economic development, home construction, and old debts, have favored primarily the new Länder.

59. For the distributional impact, and on the utilization of public commodities and services in general, see, for example K.-D. Grüske and H. D. von Loeffelholz, *Redistributionseffekte eines integrierten Finanz- und Sozialbudgets. Eine Analyse für die Bundesrepublik 1973*, Forschungsberichte des Lehrstuhls für Volkswirtschaftslehre und Finanzwissenschaft der Universität Erlangen-Nürnberg 5 (Nürnberg, 1984); W. Gillespie, *The Incidence of Taxes and Public Expenditures in the Canadian Economy: A Study Prepared for the Royal Commission on Taxation*, Report No. 6.1 (Ottawa, 1965).

60. See A. Obersteller, *Die Umverteilungswirkungen der Staatstätigkeit bei den wichtigsten Haushaltstypen. Dritter Untersuchungsteil—Eine empirische Analyse gruppenspezifischer Realtransfers*, Gutachten im Auftrag des Bundesministers für Wirtschaft (Essen: RWI, 1982), pp. 10ff.

61. For some estimates of these multipliers for the Federal Republic see, for example, H. G. Langer, J. Martiensen, and H. Quinke (eds.), *Simulationsexperimente mit ökonometrischen Makromodellen* (Munich: Oldenbourg, 1984).

62. See W. McKibbin, *The New Europe and Its Implications for the World Economy*, p. 38ff.

63. The results are displayed only graphically. The assumptions (e.g., about the long-term reduction of real wages), which are merely alluded to, do not always seem very realistic; see W. McKibbin, "Short-term Implications of Long-run Shocks: Lessons from the 1980s and 1990s," in C. Hargreaves (ed.), *Macroeconomic Modelling of the Long Run* (Brookfield, VT: 1992), pp. 21ff.

64. See the references in R. C. Bryant and others, "Design and Description of the Model Simulations," in R. C. Bryant and others (eds.), *Empirical Macroeconomics for Interdependent Economies*, pp. 3ff.

Chapter III

1. For an excellent analysis of the causes and the sectors involved see "Country Study: Germany 1994," *European Economy* (forthcoming).

2. See, for example, J. Nunes-Correia and L. Stemitsiotis, "Budget Deficit and Interest Rates: Is There a Link?—International Evidence," *Economic Papers*, vol. 105 (Brussels: European Commission, 1993). The parameters of the equation for the long-term interest rates (p. 30) are the following:

ZINSL = 3.37 + 0.51 ZINSKR + 0.68 INFLA + 0.22 DEF/GDP
(R^2 = 0.85; Durbin-Watson statistic = 1.10),

where ZINSL is the long-term interest rate, ZINSKR is the short-term real interest rate, INFLA is the inflation rate, and DEF/GDP is the ratio of the budget deficit to GNP. A 1-percentage-point increase in short-term real interest rates thus causes a rise in the long-term nominal interest rate of 0.5 percentage point, whereas a reduction in the deficit-GDP ratio by 1 percentage point leads to a decrease of 0.2 percentage point.

3. According to simulations with the RWI short-term econometric model, to compensate for the negative real GDP effects of a DM 4 billion reduction in public investment per year over three years would already require a 1-percentage-point reduction in the interest rate over this period. Similar results are obtained from the European Commission's QUEST model: see P. Bekx and others, "The QUEST Model—Version 1988," *Economic Papers*, vol. 75 (Brussels: European Commission, 1989).

4. These inflationary effects are incidentally the principal reason why the traditional theory of war finance had a strong preference for taxation. For the orthodox view on war financing see J. M. Keynes, "How to Pay for the War," *Collected Writings, IX* (MacMillan, 1972), pp. 307ff, and "Activities 1939-1945," *Collected Writings, XXII* (MacMillan, 1978), pp. 40ff.

5. According to simulations with the RWI business cycle model, an annulment of these increases and an equivalent rise of income taxes (roughly a 13.5 percent surcharge) would not only increase employment by more than 50,000 jobs in the second year, but would also reduce the government deficit by DM 2 billion a year, and reduce inflation by more than 0.3 percentage point.

6. For a detailed discussion of the fiscal and economic implications and risks of these strategies in the short and the long run, see, for example, Wissenschaftlicher Beirat beim Bundesministerium der Finanzen, "Gutachten zu den Problemen einer Verringerung der öffentlichen Netto-Neuverschuldung," *Schriftenreihe des Bundesministeriums der Finanzen* 34 (Bonn, 1984), pp. 26ff.

7. For this and the subsequent discussion see, for example, de Haan and others, *Towards Budget Discipline*, pp. 11ff., and Gebhardt, *Finanzpolitik nach dem Regierungswechsel*, p. 47ff.

8. For details of the program see Gebhardt and others, "Finanzhilfen der Bundesrepublik für die DDR," pp. 338ff.

9. The Institute of Economic Research in Halle (IWH), for example, estimates that the

"external resource requirements" of the east of DM 200 billion in 1993 will, at best, have declined by 50 percent by the year 2000; by 2005 it might drop further to DM 70 billion. To raise the living standards of the east to those in the west will take at least 20 years. The adjustment period could be reduced to 12 to 15 years only if economic growth rates of 15 percent per year are assumed; see IWH, "Neue Länder bleiben am Tropf—Transferzahlungen werden bis zum Jahr 2000 erst halbiert sein," *Börsen-Zeitung* (Frankfurt am Main, December 18, 1993, cited in Deutsche Bundesbank, *Auszüge aus Presseartikeln*, no. 91, December 21, 1993), p. 18.

10. See, for example, J. Wahse, "Arbeitsmarkt Ostdeutschland—Anpassungsszenario 2000," in K. Vogler-Ludwig (ed.), *Perspektiven für den Arbeitsmarkt in den neuen Bundesländern*, ifo-Studien zur Arbeitsmarktforschung 7 (Munich, 1991), pp. 117ff. The author projects 350,000 to 400,000 unemployed in the year 2000 (tables 2 and 3), without elaborating on these numbers and the assumed macroeconomic developments. Much more pessimistic is the *Prognos-Deutschland-Report* no. 1, which projects 955,000 unemployed in the year 2000, assuming annual GDP growth of 9.6 percent between 1992 and 2000 and GDP growth per employee of 11.1 percent. See K. Emmerich and W. Klauder, "Ein Arbeitsmarkt im Umbruch—Bestandsaufnahme und Perspektive," *IAB-Werkstattbericht* 19 (December 10, 1993), pp. 11ff, especially overview 1 and 2.

11. Some studies even rule out a GDP growth rate in the east of 7 percent annually over several years, because investment will, at best, remain at current levels, implying decreasing investment-GDP ratios, and because the marginal productivity of capital does not approach the required 17.5 percent. See "DIW: Schlechte Aussichten für hohe Wachstumsraten," *Handelsblatt*, no. 216 (November 5/6, 1993).

12. See, for example, the sample calculations in Rheinisch-Westfälisches Institut für Wirtschaftsforschung, *Konjunkturberichte*, vol. 44 (1993), p. 66.

13. They do not, however, provide a comprehensive long-term solution to the unemployment problem, because they prevent an optimal allocation of production factors, especially labor.

14. See, for example, Commission of the European Communities, *Growth, Competitiveness, Employment*, p. 9.

15. According to calculations conducted with the RWI structural model, a devaluation of the deutsche mark from 1.60 to 2.0 to the dollar would lead to an increase in the GDP growth rate of 0.1 percentage point; a reduction of the long-term real interest rate from 4.5 percent to 3.5 percent would cause a rise in GDP growth of 0.2 percentage point, and an increase in the growth of the volume of world trade by 1 percentage point would cause an increase in GDP growth of 0.3 percentage point. There even are many reasons to believe that these estimates are at the lower end of the range (see also table 2-18).

16. See, for example, W. Lamberts, "Der Einfluss von Preisänderungen auf die finanzielle Position der Gebietskörperschaften," *RWI-Mitteilungen*, vol. 28 (1977), pp. 209ff; and H. D. von Loeffelholz, "Veränderte Prioritäten im Güterangebot des Staates—Auswirkungen auf die Produktionsstruktur im Zeitraum 1960-1980," *RWI-Mitteilungen*, vol. 35 (1984), pp. 195ff.

17. The annual revenues and expenditures of the government and their annual growth rates correlate since 1960 by an average of 0.98 and 0.3, respectively. The relationship between the rates of change weakened between the time of the first oil crisis and 1977.

Until 1988 it then increased continuously, but thereafter it decreased again slightly.

18. Between 1960 and 1992 the income elasticity of public sector revenues in the Federal Republic was on average 1.13; the expenditure elasticity was 1.2.

19. For some quantifications see B. Fritzsche and others, *Perspektiven*, pp. 26ff.

20. For an economic evaluation of the importance of nonwage labor costs in the Federal Republic, see, for example, R. Döhrn, U. Heilemann, K. Löbbe, und H. D. von Loeffelholz, "Anmerkungen zum Wirtschaftsstandort Deutschland," in P. Warneke (ed.), *Wirtschaftsstandort Deutschland—Chancen und Gefahren?* Tagungsband der Sozialakademie Dortmund zur 22. Internationalen Tagung vom. 20-22 Oktober 1993 (Berlin: Duncker & Humblot, 1994), pp. 105ff.

21. See Rheinisch-Westfälisches Institut für Wirtschaftsforschung, "Stellungnahmen zum Vorschlag für eine Richtlinie des Rates zur Einführung einer Steuer auf Kohlendioxidemissionen und Energie (CO2/Energiesteuer)," submitted to a hearing of the Finance Committee of the German Bundestag, January 13, 1993, pp. 6ff.

22. See Wissenschaftlicher Beirat beim Bundesfinanzministerium, Bundesministerium der Finanzen, "Gutachten zur Reform der Gemeindesteuern," *Schriftenreihe des Bundesministeriums der Finanzen* 31 (Bonn, 1982).

23. See H. D. von Loeffelholz, "Struktureffekte einer 'Maschinensteuer'—Eine Modellanalyse zur Umbasierung des Arbeitgeberanteils an den Sozialversicherungsbeiträgen," *RWI-Mitteilungen*, vol. 34 (1983), pp. 229ff, and W. Schmähl, H.-D. Henke, and H. M. Schellhaaß, *Änderungen der Beitragsfinanzierung in der "Maschinenbeitrags"* (Baden-Baden: Nomos, 1984).

24. Contributions to unemployment insurance are shared equally by employers and employees.

25. See Bundesministerium der Finanzen, *Bericht der Bundesregierung über die Entwicklung der Finanzhilfen des Bundes und der Steuervergünstigungen für die Jahre 1991 bis 1994*, Vierzehnter Subventionsbericht (Bonn, 1993), pp. 28ff.

26. Losses in tax revenues resulting from the basic tax exemption amount to about DM 40 billion annually, those resulting from child allowances to about DM 12 billion, and the deductible for retirement planning to about DM 15 billion. In limiting these exemptions it is necessary to consider the feedback effects, which are likely to reduce the additional tax revenues mentioned here by one-quarter to one-third.

27. If apartment rents were taxed at half the current sales tax rate of 7 percent, or at the entire rate of 15 percent, additional revenues—*ceteris paribus*—of DM 7 billion or DM 15 billion, respectively, would accrue.

28. The proposal of a local value-added tax is aimed at this aspect, which would also include professionals and public administrations.

29. For the respective proposals, see, for example, B. Fritzsche, U. Heilemann, and H. D. von Loeffelholz, "Überlegungen zur Finanzierung der 'Grossen Steuerreform,'" *RWI-Mitteilungen*, vol. 36/37 (1986/87), pp. 38ff.

30. For the position of the Federal Republic in the context of the European Union until 1989 see de Haan and others, *Towards Budget Discipline*, pp. 21ff.

31. The reduction of tax benefits with a concomitant decrease in tax rates would be politically counterproductive considering the intended maximization of votes, because those affected by the limitation of tax possibilities are more politically influential than

those who benefit most from the reduction of tax rates. See, for example, Organization for Economic Cooperation and Development, *Tax Expenditures: A Review of the Issues and Country Practices* (Paris, 1984).

32. Starting in 1995 this surcharge is likely to be reactivated at a rate of 7.5 percent. It will lead initially to additional tax revenues of DM 28 billion annually. The principal alternative, which has been proposed often in the context of a labor market contribution by civil servants, is a 10 percent additional surcharge on middle and higher incomes only. According to the Ministry of Finance this surcharge could only match the amount raised by the 7.5 percent solidarity surcharge if it started at gross income levels of DM 44,000 for single and DM 94,200 for married households with two children. This corresponds to annual taxable incomes of DM 38,000 and DM 76,000, respectively. If the surcharge were to start at the average gross yearly income of about DM 51,000 (corresponding to DM 45,000 and DM 90,000 taxable income), a revenue loss of DM 3.5 billion annually would accrue. See Bundesministerium der Finanzen, *BMF-Finanznachrichten*, no. 18/94 (March 15, 1994), p. 1ff.

33. This includes the increase in the motor vehicle tax for gasoline-powered cars.

34. See Organization for Economic Cooperation and Development, *Revenue Statistics 1965-1993*, p. 85. This includes essentially the wealth tax and the transfer tax (e.g., the inheritance, gift, and realty transfer taxes).

35. For the situation in the mid-1980s see, for example, H. D. Loeffelholz, "Die Standortqualität der Bundesrepublik in steuerlicher Hinsicht," *RWI-Mitteilungen*, vol. 39 (1988), pp. 194ff. For the changes in Germany's competitiveness from a tax perspective in recent years see K. Löbbe and others, *Strukturwandel in der Krise*, pp. 56ff.

36. With respect to growth and competition policy considerations, tax increases that inhibit income generation (direct taxes) appear to be more problematic than those that affect consumption, and than transfer taxes (indirect taxes).

37. In the new Länder these structures still need to be established in the years to come. This applies in particular to the areas of transportation, communication, and waste management. Bringing the infrastructural elements up to par is especially important for reducing the still-existing investment impediments for private and public capital.

38. See Deutsche Bundesbank, *Aufkommen und ökonomische Auswirkungen des steuerlichen Zinsabschlags*, pp. 45ff.

39. This estimate is based on the assumption that about 10 percent of the national product is generated in the black economy, or about DM 320 billion per year. With overall taxes and contributions at 44.5 percent of GNP, the fisci would incur losses of about DM 150 billion.

40. See R. Döhrn, "Wie gross ist die Schattenwirtschaft—Versuch einer sektoralen Erklärung," *RWI-Mitteilungen*, vol. 37/38 (1986/87), pp. 365ff. Here the size of the black economy in the early 1980s is estimated to have been between 2.5 percent and 5 percent of GNP. Under current conditions this equals about DM 80 billion to DM 160 billion, half of which would represent lost government revenues.

41. See H. Rappen and B. Fritzsche, *Gesamtwirtschaftliche Kosten staatlicher Ausgabe- und Einnahmeentscheidungen—dargestellt am Beispiel der Bundesrepublik Deutschland*, Gutachten im Auftrag des Bundesministers der Finanzen (Essen: RWI, 1988), pp. 10ff.

42.   Rheinisch-Westfälisches Institut für Wirtschaftsforschung, *RWI-Konjunkturberichte*, vol. 44 (1993), p. 216.

43. Between 1983 and the end of 1988 the government received DM 6.6 billion through the sale of stocks and preemptive rights; see Bundesministerium der Finanzen, *40 Jahre Verantwortung für die Finanzen des Bundes. Das Bundesministerium der Finanzen—Geschichte, Aufgaben, Leistungen* (Munich: Olzog, 1989), pp. 170ff. For a critical appraisal of the privatization policy since 1982, see H. Tofaute, *Der grosse Ausverkauf. Die Privatisierung der Bundesunternehmen durch die Regierung Kohl* (Cologne: Bund, 1994).

44. For a comprehensive overview of federal investments see Bundesministerium der Finanzen, *Beteiligungen des Bundes im Jahr 1993*.

45. See Bundesministerium der Finanzen, *Finanzbericht 1994*, pp. 48ff.

46. This compulsory investment aid, which generated DM 1.2 billion annually, amounted to 5 percent of income taxes owed and had to be paid by taxpayers with annual taxable incomes over DM 50,000 for singles and DM 100,000 for married couples. Taxpayers who invested five times as much as their contribution in their enterprise were exempted. The measure was declared unconstitutional by Germany's constitutional court on November 6, 1984. See also R. Hickel and J. Priewe, *Nach dem Fehlstart. Ökonomische Perspektiven der deutschen Einigung* (Frankfurt am Main: Fischer, 1994), pp. 206ff, although this source makes no mention of the possible additional revenue that could be raised.

47. See, for example, Boskin, *Reagan and the Economy*, p. 235.

48. See, for example, Boskin, *Reagan and the Economy*, pp. 219ff., and, most recently, Economic Report of the President, 1994, pp. 78ff.

49. See, for example, N. Crafts, "Productivity Growth Reconsidered," *Economic Policy*, vol. 75. (1992), pp. 38ff. Crafts examines the contributions of new growth theories in light of the European experience since World War II.

50. See E. Denison, *Accounting for U.S. Economic Growth, 1929-69* (Brookings, 1974), pp. 84ff. and 149ff., and Rheinisch-Westfälisches Institut für Wirtschaftsforschung, *Analyse der strukturellen Entwicklung der deutschen Wirtschaft—RWI-Strukturberichterstattung 1987*, vols. 1 and 5 (Essen: RWI, 1988).

51. For the United States, A. Blinder has argued that an increase in the share of investment in GNP by 3 percentage points for one decade—a considerable rise—would increase the growth rate of the capital stock by 1 percentage point. After 10 years this amounts to an increase of the capital stock by 10.5 percent. The growth rate of real GNP would increase as a consequence by a remarkable 3.15 percent, although the real GNP growth rate would rise by only 0.12 percentage point within a 25-year time period; see A. Blinder, "Reaganomics and Growth," in C. Hulton and I. Sawhill (eds.), *The Legacy of Reaganomics* (Urban Institute Press, 1984), cited in M. Boskin, *Reagan and the Economy*, p. 234.

52. See A. Peacock and J. Wiseman, *The Growth of Public Expenditures in the United Kingdom* (Princeton University Press, 1961), pp. 24ff. On the importance of these effects for the public budgets see A. Wildavsky, *The Politics of the Budgetary Process*, p. 124. Wildavsky points to the many difficulties of putting up with changing demands in the (fiscal) political process.

53. See Bundesministerium der Finanzen, "Die deutsche Einheit und das öffentliche Defizit—ein lösbares Problem," *BMF-Finanznachrichten*, vol. 65/93 (October 27, 1993), p. 4. The growth in expenditures at all government levels is supposed to be "strictly" limited: "The budgets in the medium term should grow by only 2.3 percent, that is, only at half the rate as nominal GNP." This implies that the government share in GNP would drop from its current 51.5 percent to 45.5 percent over the next five years. See also below.

54. See H. Gebhardt, U. Heilemann, and H. D. von Loeffelholz, "Finanzhilfen der Bundesrepublik für die DDR: Umfang, Formen, Wirkungen," *RWI-Mitteilungen*, vol. 40 (1989), p. 333.

55. The fiscal plans do not disclose the interest rate on which the future growth of interest payments is based.

56. See Bundesministerium der Finanzen, *Perspektiven staatlicher Ausgabenpolitik. Gutachten erstattet vom Wissenschaftlichen Beirat beim Bundesministerium der Finanzen*, Schriftenreihe des Bundesministerium der Finanzen 51 (Bonn, 1994), pp. 60ff. The analysis, however, omits any quantification of the savings potential.

57. A case study of the state budget of Lower Saxony concluded that a productivity realization equal to the average for the western German Länder would lead to annual savings of DM 600 billion; see H. D. von Loeffelholz und H. Rappen, *Perspektiven und Optionen niedersächsischer Finanzpolitik in den neunziger Jahren*, Untersuchungen des Rheinisch-Westfälischen Institut für Wirtschaftsforschung 11 (Essen: RWI, forthcoming).

58. See K. Löbbe and others, *Strukturwandel in der Krise*, pp. 227ff. Between 1982 and 1989 the public sector share of GNP was reduced by 0.5 percentage point; see Bundesministerium der Finanzen, *Bericht der Bundesregierung über die Finanzhilfen des Bundes und der Steuervergünstigungen für die Jahre 1991 bis 1994*, p. 13.

Chapter IV

1. See de Haan and others, *Towards Budget Discipline*, pp. 36ff.

2. The empirical results of de Haan and others (*Towards Budget Discipline*, p. 43) regarding the impact of the above-mentioned factors on the differences in public indebtedness in the EU countries between 1981 and 1989 is not very convincing. It is noteworthy, however, that in light of these determinants the conditions for the financing of unification were extremely favorable.

3. For the different expenditure and deficit patterns among the western German Länder during the last 20 years see H. D. von Loeffelholz and H. Rappen, *Perspektiven und Optionen*, pp. 55ff.

4. See Wildavsky, *The Politics of the Budgetary Process*, pp. 63ff.

5. Diminished government activities have the tendency to redistribute from the "(not very) poor to the (not very) rich," especially if the reduction of monetary and real transfers is realized in the areas of social security, health care, or education. For some empirical evidence on the leveling of these redistributional effects see, for example, K.-D. Grüske and H. D. von Loeffelholz, *Redistributionseffekte eines integrierten Finanz- und Sozialbudgets*, pp. 10ff.

6. See R. Döhrn and others, *Anmerkungen*, pp. 10ff.; K. Löbbe and others, *Strukturwandel in der Krise*, pp. 56ff.

7. See Rheinisch-Westfälisches Institut für Wirtschaftsforschung, *Konjunkturberichte*, vol. 44 (1993), pp. 151ff.

8. The same applies to the increased strain on the EU budget and, indirectly, on the German budget due to plans by the European Commission, outlined in its recent White Paper, to develop trans-European networks. See U. Heilemann and H. D. von Loeffelholz, "Wachstum durch Transeuropäische Netze? Zum Infrastrukturprogramm des Weissbuchs," in H. König (ed.), *Das Weissbuch der EU-Kommission* (Baden-Baden: Nomos, forthcoming).

9. This does not even get into the question of whether the government has a legal obligation to reduce taxes. Without going into detail, we may note that the experience in the Federal Republic indicates that so far it has not been necessary to resolve this issue, but also that there are no judicial means of enforcing such an obligation, if it exists.

10. In public it is often argued that, for procedural reasons, the surcharge will have to be reevaluated after three years. But according to a decision by Germany's supreme court in 1972, there are no legal instruments for setting a time limit on a solidarity surcharge; see "Die Ergänzungsabgabe ist mit dem Grundgesetz vereinbar," *Monatsschrift für Deutsches Recht*, vol. 26 (1972), p. 759.

11. On January 1, 1968, a 3 percent surcharge on personal and corporate income taxes was introduced for taxable incomes above DM 16,000 and DM 32,000, for single and married individuals respectively. Although they were revoked as separate federal taxes (the former on January 1, 1975, and the latter on January 1, 1977), they were included in the context of the reform of income tax structures in the same year as their annulment.

12. For some of those proposals see *Die Lage der Weltwirtschaft und der Deutschen Wirtschaft im Frühjahr 1994*. Beurteilung der Wirtschaftslage durch folgende Mitglieder der Arbeitsgemeinschaft deutscher wirtschaftswissenschaftlicher Forschungsinstitute e.V., München: Deutsches Institut für Wirtschaftsforschung, Berlin, HWWA-Institut für Wirtschaftsforschung, Hamburg, ifo Institut für Wirtschaftsforschung, München, Institut für Weltwirtschaft an der Universität Kiel, Institut für Wirtschaftsforschung, Halle, Rheinisch-Westfälisches Institut für Wirtschaftsforschung, Essen, München, 1994, p. 24.

13. Such a policy should be pursued despite the previous practice between 1964 and 1975, and between 1981 and 1986, when the combination of unchanged income tax rates and inflation led to substantial revenues from hidden taxes; see B. Fritzsche, U. Heilemann, and H. D. von Loeffelholz, "Was bringt die Steuerreform? *Wirtschaftsdienst*, vol. 65 (1985), pp. 471ff.

14. Estimates based on table 2-9 above and Statistisches Bundesamt, *Konten und Standardtabellen 1992. Hauptbericht. Fachserie 18: Volkswirtschaftliche Gesamtrechnungen*, Reihe 1.3 (Stuttgart, 1993), pp. 247ff.

15. See also "Reserven des IMF-Stabes gegenüber Maastricht—Zu hoher Preis für die Erfüllung der Konvergenzkriterien," *Neue Zürcher Zeitung* (July 31, 1992). The results of the IMF study (which were initially to be published in *World Economic Outlook 1992* but were subsequently cancelled) were criticized by the European Commission. However, other studies have come to similar conclusions in the case of Germany, where real GNP is expected to remain 1.5 percent below what it would otherwise be between 1992 and 1999; for Italy the GNP shortfall is expected to be as much as 5 percent; France and the United Kingdom would be only indirectly affected via trade and monetary effects. No

negative implications are expected for the world economy, since the anticipated lower interest rates would more than counteract these developments; see A. Giovanni and W. McKibbin, *The Economic Consequences of Maastricht* (Brookings, 1992), pp. 8ff.